GW00504659

MoviePlus X3
Director's Guide

The Director's Guide was created and output using Serif PagePlus.

How to contact us

Contacting Serif technical support

Our support mission is to provide fast, friendly technical advice and support from a team of on-call experts. Technical support is provided from our web support page, and useful information can be obtained via our web-based forums (see below). There are no pricing policies after the 30 day money back guarantee period.

UK/International/
US Technical Support :   http://www.serif.com/support

Additional Serif contact information

Web:

Serif Web Site: http://www.serif.com

Forums: http://www.serif.com/forums.asp

Main office (UK, Europe):

The Software Centre, PO Box 2000, Nottingham, NG11 7GW, UK

Main:	(0115) 914 2000
Registration (UK only):	(0800) 376 1989
Sales (UK only):	(0800) 376 7070
Customer Service (UK/International):	http://www.serif.com/support
General Fax:	(0115) 914 2020

North American office (US, Canada):

The Software Center, 13 Columbia Drive, Suite 5, Amherst NH 03031, USA

Main:	(603) 889-8650
Registration:	(800) 794-6876
Sales:	(800) 55-SERIF or 557-3743
Customer Service:	http://www.serif.com/support
General Fax:	(603) 889-1127

International enquiries

Please contact our main office.

Introduction

Welcome to the **MoviePlus X3 Director's Guide**! Whether you are
new to MoviePlus or a seasoned filmmaker, this guide offers content to
help you get the best out of the program.

Our aim is to demystify what can often be a complex process, and show
you how to use your digital video equipment in conjunction with
MoviePlus. You'll find advice and tips on planning your project, editing your
footage, applying professional movie-editing techniques, and sharing your
finished movie.

Whatever your level of expertise, we hope you'll find this guide a valuable
resource that will help you create movies you can be proud of.

The guide is organized into the following chapters:

- **Chapter 1: The Basics**

  Guides you through the main stages of the movie-making process—
  from planning your project, right through to sharing your finished
  movie.

- **Chapter 2: Tips and Tricks**

  Describes some of the events that you're most likely to want to shoot,
  and provides general guidelines to help you do so successfully—the first
  time!

- **Chapter 3: Timeline Techniques**

  A collection of fully-illustrated, step-by-
  step tutorials designed to help you get
  the most out of the rich functionality
  provided by MoviePlus.

   For information on
  working in Storyboard mode,
  see the **How To** pane and
  online Help.

  These exercises focus on the
  techniques we think you'll find most
  useful, and cover a wide range of
  movie-editing techniques that can be
  accomplished in Timeline mode.

- **Chapter 4: DVD/VCD Menu Templates**

  A useful reference gallery showing full-colour previews of the
  DVD/VCD menu templates included with MoviePlus X3.

Contents

The Basics

This chapter guides you through the main stages of the movie-making process with the aim of helping you produce the best possible results.

From planning and shooting your video, right through to editing your footage, we'll discuss the key elements that will help to make your project a success.

Planning Your Project

Shooting a video is not a simple process and there are many things to consider if you want to produce professional looking results.

Before you begin filming, it's important to take some time to plan and prepare for your project. The following sections outline some of the fundamental principles that will help to make your project a success.

Decide on your story and how you want to tell it

It sounds obvious, but it's surprising how many people end up shooting aimlessly with no overall 'narrative thread' to hold the finished video or film together.

🎬 Telling your story

If you're filming a video of your family holiday for example, begin by shooting some scenes of family members preparing for the trip.

- Capture them packing their suitcases and include a shot of the family before you leave.

- Include shots en route to your destination—the packed car or taxi, the plane at the boarding gate, and so on.

- Include footage of the return journey, children sleeping in the car, sunburned faces, waiting for the luggage at the carousel, etc.

💡 Why create a storyboard?

A storyboard is a visual script or plan of the scenes and scene changes in a series of video shots. While this step is an important one, many people ignore it and jump right into filming instead. So why is it so important?

- Creating a storyboard helps you to think about how you want your finished film to look, how the story should unfold, and what shots will best convey your story to the viewer.

- Storyboarding is especially useful for planning complex sequences of events, saving you from missing essential footage or shooting footage you can't use.

Your storyboard should include sketches of the most important scenes, notes about dialogue, sound effects, location, and so on.

Think about the story you want to tell, and the way in which you want it to unfold. This is a basic principle, but one that distinguishes between boring haphazard footage that will send your audience to sleep, and a movie that will hold their attention.

Your production will naturally fall into one of two types: **scripted** or **unscripted**.

Scripted

This category includes movies and animated films. If you're filming an interview, the interviewer's questions will be scripted, while the answers obviously won't be. However, you can sometimes predict the type of response a question is likely to generate, which can be helpful in determining the flow of conversation and the way in which one question leads to another.

Unscripted

This category includes documentary style films, news segments, and 'home videos' covering events such as weddings, vacations, birthday parties, and so on.

Visit the location

If you can, it's always a good idea to visit the location of your shoot beforehand so that you can plan your camera positions.

If you're shooting an event such as a wedding, you won't have any say in the location (unless it's your own wedding, in which case you should ask someone else to do the filming for you!), but you might still be able to check it out in advance.

If you're filming your family vacation, however, you obviously won't be able to do this. Even so, you can still think about the location and the types of shots you think you'll need.

Location checklist

The following list outlines the most important things to check on a location 'recce':

- Is there enough light? If your shoot is taking place indoors, note the location of the windows. If you're shooting outside, think about the position of the sun at various times of the day.

- Is it quiet enough? Make a note of any background noise that might interfere with the audio recording.

- Is there enough space? Plan where you will position your subjects and the camera, keeping in mind the background and light source.

- If you need a power source, locate the nearest power outlet.

- In exterior locations, look for possible cover in case of adverse weather conditions.

- Note how busy the site is at various times of the day.

- Do you need permission to film there? Are you on private property? If you need permission, it's best to get it in writing.

- Locate the nearest car park— particularly important if you're using a lot of heavy equipment, or if you're using actors.

Get to know your equipment

Before you begin shooting, make sure you are familiar with your equipment (you might even want to read your manuals!).

It's a good idea to shoot a few hours of practice footage, rehearsing all the things you think you'll need to do.

Practise using your tripod and microphone. You can even try various lighting techniques to see the different effects you can achieve.

Experiment

New techniques take practice and experimentation. Note any techniques or shots you'd like to try, and then experiment at a time when it doesn't matter—not during a wedding video shoot, for example!

🔍 Equipment tips

- Buy good tapes

Use good quality tapes from a reputable manufacturer. Cheap tapes are less robust and more likely to break.

- Use a head cleaner

Camcorder and MiniDV tapes deposit a layer of ferric oxide on the tape heads, forming a barrier between them and the tape. This layer builds up and ultimately reduces film quality by causing lines and obstructions to appear on the tape. A head cleaner removes this residue from the tape heads. For optimum performance, you should clean your tape heads regularly—once a month is advisable.

Storyboarding

Storyboarding is the process of creating a visual script, or plan, of the shots and scene changes in a video or film.

Storyboards are invaluable when several people are working on a project together. A well-defined storyboard helps to ensure that everyone understands the goals of the project and how the video and audio footage should work together.

This section explains the storyboarding process, outlines the most common items found on a storyboard, and aims to provide guidelines for you to create your own.

You may find some sections too detailed for your purposes, or you may decide you need to include some additional elements in your storyboard.

Whatever type of production you're planning, bear in mind that the more detailed and specific your storyboard, generally the easier the production and post-production phases will be.

You don't have to be an artist to create an effective storyboard—rough sketches of stick figures will do just as well.

While these examples vary stylistically, they all include the essential information. Try to include as much detail as possible about the scenes you want to shoot. Keep in mind also that a storyboard is a 'live document' and will change and evolve as your ideas develop.

The storyboarding process is an important one for the following reasons:

- To deliver its message effectively, a video or film production needs to be well planned.

  Storyboarding helps you to think about how you want your finished film to look, how the story should unfold, and what shots will best convey your story to your audience.

- With your storyboard in place, you'll waste less time setting up shots because you'll know exactly what scenes you need to shoot, and where to shoot them from.

- Storyboarding is especially useful for planning complex sequences of events, saving you from shooting footage you can't use or missing footage that is essential to the plot.

Components

When creating a storyboard, think of your video as a story comprising various elements in a timeline. For each major scene, you should include information about who the subject is, what they are doing, where and why they are doing it, and so on.

If you know the location where you will be shooting, it's a good idea to sketch a rough plan view showing the placement of the camera, light source, people, and any other important features or props.

Include sketches of important scenes, along with scene descriptions, and notes about location, transitions, plot, dialogue, and sound effects.

Synopsis

At the top of your storyboard, write a short paragraph outlining the story or event that your video is going to capture. You could also include character profiles and any other issues related to the story.

Sketch

This area is for sketching a rough representation of the main scenes that you want to capture during shooting.

Your sketches do not have to be detailed, but must be accurate enough so that you understand the type of shot required.

For example, there should be no chance of taking a long shot when you need a close-up.

You might want to start by including a sketch of your establishing shot. This will set the scene for your audience and provide information about the location of your story. You could then cut to a medium shot to introduce your subject.

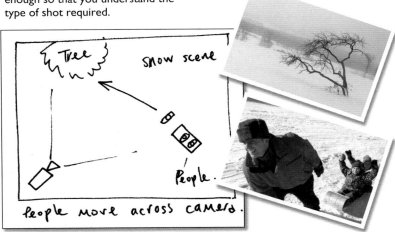

Shot description

This section contains a description about what needs to be captured in the shot—specifically, anything that is difficult to explain in a single sketch.

For example, you might want to specify:

- The **estimated time of take**: How long (in seconds) you anticipate this segment will be. During shooting, this will help you to make sure that your long segments are long enough. During editing, it will help you determine which sections need to be shortened.

  It's best to use longer shots for complex scenes and shorter shots for close-ups.

- The **camera shot** required: Do you want this shot to be a close up, or an extreme close up? For information about different camera shots, see "Shot types" (p. 18).

- The **camera angle** required: For example, is this an aerial shot, an eye-level angle shot, a tilting shot? See "Shot angles" (p. 22).

Shot sequence number

You may think that the sequence of your shots is obvious. However, when you've added all the main elements of your storyboard, we suggest you assign each shot a sequence number.

As your ideas develop, you may decide to change the order of your shots. You'll find these sequence numbers invaluable when you come to edit your footage.

Transition in and out

Identify your scene transitions— how you move from one shot to the next—in your storyboard. This will make the editing phase much easier, and will help you to determine if you have enough variation between shots.

For example, if you have the same type of shots following each other (a medium shot followed by another similar medium shot), you need to ensure that this won't be confusing for your audience.

You should also compare the transition 'out' of one shot with the following transition 'in' of the next shot. Generally, if you use a particular transition to take the viewer out of a scene, don't use a similar transition to lead into the next scene.

Script

You may not need this section, but it's important to include it if you want a subject or narrator to follow a specific script during a particular scene.

If you're recording an interview, make a note of the questions to be asked and the responses you anticipate.

Recorded audio

As you capture your video footage, you can also simultaneously record your audio. If you're using an external microphone, make a note of when it should be used. You should also note any scenes in which you don't want any sound recorded, and those where background audio is required.

For example, at a track and field event, you might want to record the sound of the starter's gun, some crowd noise, applause, and so on.

Secondary audio

If you want to add secondary audio to a scene during editing, make a note of it too. For example, in addition to the audio recorded during shooting, you might also want to include music, a voice-over, sound effects, or another audio track.

And that's all there is to it...

We've covered the major elements that are generally found on project storyboards. Keep in mind, however, that there are no strict rules for creating storyboards—each one will differ depending on the project it illustrates.

Shooting Techniques

When shooting video footage, there are some basic principles that can make a big difference and will help you to produce better quality raw footage and ultimately, professional-looking results.

Tips and tricks

There are many things to consider if you want to produce good quality raw footage. The following section provides some guidelines.

Position your camcorder–and yourself!

Unless you have a very steady hand, use a tripod to ensure steady pictures. If using a tripod, make sure it's stable and level. If you don't have a tripod, use a wall, door frame, or any stable structure for support.

You'll increase your stability by using the camcorder's hand or neck strap (or both), and by holding the camcorder securely against your head and eye so that it moves with your body. Keep your arms close to your body with one hand on the camcorder body and the other near the 'Record' button.

Visualise your shot before setting up, then choose your position relative to the background and where the action will take place.

Shoot everything!

Capture everything you can. You can edit as much as you want later, but it's better to have lots of footage to choose from.

Press Record before the shot begins

To make sure you capture everything, start shooting about 20 seconds or so before the shot really begins.

Check the location

Look for different or creative locations as these can really add impact to the shot.

> Some camcorders don't start to record as soon as you press the Record button, so you should allow a couple of seconds extra.

Consider your light source

Before you begin shooting your video, take a look at where the light is coming from.

To avoid turning your video subjects into shadows, shoot with the light source behind you, rather than behind your subject. Whenever possible, use natural light.

Choose backgrounds carefully

Avoid background clutter and objects that could merge with your subject to create distracting effects—such as a tree that appears to 'grow' out of a person's head!

Turn off the date/time stamp

You don't need to have the time and date displayed throughout your video.

Generally, this feature will interfere with your edits and reduce the visual impact of your movie. Most digital camcorders let you turn this feature off at any time after recording.

Don't use autofocus

While autofocus is useful for giving certain images a crisp effect, for maximum control you should turn it off and focus manually instead.

Turn off camcorder effects

While it might be tempting to use your camcorder's built-in features (such as scene transition effects like auto fade), you should turn these off. Instead, concentrate on taking good quality standard footage—you can add any effects you want during editing.

Never use autofocus when shooting footage in which your subjects are moving, when there's little contrast between subject and background, or when filming through elements such as windows, fences, trees, etc.

In these situations, autofocus will not be able to determine which elements are meant to be in focus and will shift between the foreground and the background, so you need to identify the subject for the camcorder.

Rehearse difficult shots

Practice taking any difficult shots beforehand, especially those that require tricky camcorder techniques such as panning.

Break it up

Rather than filming in one continuous take, divide the scene up into separate shots.

Any activity can be broken down into individual moments in time. The secret of good video shooting is being able to identify these, and thus divide a complete action into a series of separate shots.

During the editing phase, you can decide which shots to keep and which ones to discard.

Use slow, smooth motion

A common mistake beginners make is to zoom in and out a lot. This can be very distracting for the audience.

While there are times when you might want to zoom, these types of shots should be kept to a minimum.

If you must pan a scene, move the camcorder smoothly and slowly (or follow some action to establish the scene, rather than just panning a scene with no action).

Avoid the 'firehose effect'—trying to capture the action in several different places by quickly jerking the camcorder around.

You'll find more tips on shooting moving subjects later in this section.

> If you need to capture a scene from different angles or with a different zoom setting, stop recording, move to a different position or change your zoom setting, and then continue shooting.

Wait before moving

After you've finished recording, wait a second or two before you move to ensure that your shots don't end with distracting jerky movement.

Think about audio

The audio track is just as important to your final movie as the video footage. Before you start filming, check to make sure you're getting an audio feed.

While you're recording, think about what's happening to the sound.

For example, are there any extraneous background noises that might be distracting?

You might want to record some background audio separately, and then add it to your movie during the editing process. Adding background sound as a separate audio track ensures that your movie's soundtrack is consistent.

For more information and tips on recording sound, see "Audio Recording" (p. 33).

Shot types

To create an interesting video, you need to include a variety of different types of shots. Shots are commonly divided up into the following categories:

Extreme close-up (ECU)

Extreme close-ups focus on a particular part of a person—mouth, eyes, hands, etc. Use these shots to create a feeling of intimacy in your video, and to convey a mood or emotion. These shots are very intense, so use them sparingly. The ECU is too close to show general reactions or emotion except in very dramatic scenes.

Close-up (CU)

Close-up shots typically contain just the face of a subject. These can also convey a real sense of emotion and help the audience to connect with the subject.

Medium close-up (MCU)

Medium close-ups show the subject's face more clearly, but do not get as close as the close-up.

Medium shot (MS)

Medium shots (or mid shots) typically frame subjects from the waist up. These shots tend to be used the most in a film production. They portray the audience's everyday perception of people. The MS is appropriate when the subject is speaking or delivering information without much emotion.

Two-shot or three-shot (2-S or 3-S)

Often medium shots, these are shots of two or three people in one scene. They are often used in interviews and are also good for establishing a relationship between subjects.

Extreme wide shot (EWS)

Extreme wide shots are far removed from the subject and often shot with a wide-angle lens. They may show the subject in the distance, but the emphasis is more on showing the subject in his or her environment.

Point of view shot (POV)

Also called a subjective shot. The camcorder adopts the perspective of a character. We see what a character sees and therefore identify with him/her. The person whose point of view it is should never be seen in the shot. These shots are often used to add drama in chase scenes.

Wide shot (WS)

Wide shots (also known as long shots) provide an overall view of the whole scene. If the shot contains a person, the whole body is shown.

Over-the-shoulder shot (OSS)

These shots look at the subject from behind a person. They show the back of a person's head (often cutting off the frame just behind the ear) and sometimes one shoulder.

Reaction shot

Also known as noddy shots, these shots show a person's face listening or reacting to something. Reaction shots are common in interviews and are also often used to cut into a sequence.

Establishing shot

Usually a wide shot or an extreme wide shot, which sets the scene at the beginning of a film or section of film and shows where the action is taking place.

Cutaway (CA)

Placed between the main shots, a cutaway is usually of something other than the current action. These shots are used as transitions between main shots, or to add interest or information. For example, a typical CA shot could be a close up of the subject's mouth or hands—also known as a cut-in (CI), or a shot of an entirely different subject.

Shot angles

The shot angle is the level from which you look at your subject through the camcorder.

As a general rule, shoot people at head height.

Try to vary the shot angle as much as possible as you may find an unusual view that will add interest to your movie. You're also guaranteed to end up with a greater variety of footage to work with when editing.

Eye-level angle

Because this is the perspective most familiar to us, the eye-level angle is one of the most commonly used shots. If you want to shoot at this angle, however, bear in mind that 'eye-level' refers to your subject's eye level—not yours.

High angle

In these shots, the camcorder looks down on the subject making it appear smaller and less important. High angle shots are often used to make a person appear vulnerable.

Low angle

In low angle shots, the camcorder looks up at the subject. Use these shots when you want to make your subject appear larger, imposing, or more important to the viewer.

Don't just stick to the basic shot angles though. Be adventurous and experiment with shot angles and perspective...

Tilting shot

Experiment with panning in the vertical plane instead of the horizontal.

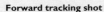

Aerial shot

Shoot an establishing shot from above.

Forward tracking shot

Try shooting a moving subject from behind.

When shooting subjects that are close to the ground, get down on the same level.

If you're crouching, use your knee to balance the camcorder; for very low shots, lie on the ground and use your elbows for support. Most camcorders have eyepieces that you can adjust for easier viewing angles.

If your subject is a child, get down on their level; the results will be much more effective than filming from yours.

Composition and framing

Before you start shooting, take a good look at your shot. Do you have everything that you want in the shot? Is the shot framed well? The following tips will help you create balanced, professional-looking footage.

Balance your composition

Look at the shapes and the colours in the shot. They should create a balanced picture and draw attention to the subject, rather than drawing the eye away from it. If you're not happy with the way your shot is set up, try taking it from another position or angle.

Think about backgrounds

A good background should be neutral or should compliment the video subject; it should not overwhelm it or distract from it.

Examples of distracting backgrounds can often be seen in live television interviews, shot on location, where people are waving and jumping around behind the reporter.

Make sure your subjects are looking into the frame

If there are people in your shot, they should generally be looking towards the centre of the frame. For example, if you're filming a person who is looking to the left, position them in the right of the frame.

Use the 'rule of thirds'

When setting up a composition, use the rule of thirds for more interesting shots.

Simply put, this rule states that if you divide your frame roughly into thirds, horizontally and vertically, any points where those lines intersect is a good place to position your main subject.

Placing your subject in the centre of the shot will create a much less interesting composition.

Use perspective and look for natural frames

Use perspective to draw your audience into an image.

Shoot your subjects inside frames—for example, a building through an archway or a person in a doorway.

Vary shot lengths

Your movie will be more interesting if you vary your shot lengths. For example, use longer shots for establishing shots (to set the scene) and for complex shots such as a busy street scene; use shorter shots for close ups and reaction shots.

Move between shots

In most cases, you should not follow one shot with another similar shot.

The reason for this is continuity—to present a seamless narration, you don't want your audience to be consciously aware of (and distracted by) cuts and transitions between scenes.

For example, if a shot containing a person or object is followed by another similarly framed shot, it creates the appearance that the subject is quickly 'jumping' from one position to another.

Don't cross the line!

Known as the '180 degree rule,' this standard rule of filmmaking states that the camcorder should always stay on one side of the subjects (or action) in a scene. To help you visualise this, imagine a line cutting through the middle of the scene—the camcorder should never cross this line.

For example, when shooting a scene showing a person walking from left to right, the imaginary line runs across the scene on the subject's left side. If you were to move to the other side of the line and continue to shoot, the scene would be reversed and your subject would now be walking from right to left.

This change of orientation would appear strange and confusing to the viewer.

To avoid making this mistake, you should try to set up your scene and subjects so that you can shoot all from the same side.

💡 There are some situations in which crossing the line is unavoidable. In these cases, take a shot right on the 'line' itself and then use this as a transition to 'guide' your audience to the new orientation.

Watch for headroom, looking room, and lead space

These terms refer to the amount of room in the frame which is purposely left empty.

- **Headroom** is the amount of space between the top of the subject's head and the top of the frame. Leaving too much headroom wastes frame space and makes your subject appear to be sinking. In a close up, too little headroom draws the viewer's eye to the chin and neck, rather than the eyes.

- **Looking room** is the amount of space left in the direction the subject is looking. When shooting one person talking to another—the person on the left should be framed to the left of centre, the other person to the right. If you're shooting a subject who is talking directly to camcorder—place the subject to the left or right of centre.

- **Lead space** refers to the space in front of a moving subject, for example a person walking or a moving vehicle. This may also be referred to as **nose room**, or **look space**. Without adequate lead space, the frame will look awkward.

Use a dolly to shoot a moving subject

There will be times when you'll want to shoot a moving subject. These shots are particularly tricky if you're using a handheld camcorder as it's difficult to keep it level and steady.

Professionals use **dollies**—camcorder supports with wheels—for this purpose. Purpose-made dollies are very expensive, but you can make your own using virtually anything with wheels. For example, you could use a pushchair, wheelchair, or shopping trolley.

Make sure your 'dolly' moves smoothly and without noise, then secure your tripod and camcorder inside it. Before shooting, check the scene through the camcorder, and then adjust the tripod until you've achieved the shooting level you need.

You can now film your subjects in one of the following ways:

- By walking behind them.
- By walking beside them.
- By walking backwards, in front of them—be careful!

Focus

Your camcorder's automatic focus mode will work fine for shooting scenes where your subject is well and evenly lit, and in which there is contrast between the subject and the background. However, for all other situations, you'll need to be comfortable using manual focus.

Beginners often have problems when trying to shoot a night scene that contains bright objects, such as car headlights. Here, the automatic focus will centre on the car headlights as soon as they enter the scene, causing the focus of the subject to be lost.

The following technique will help you keep the subject of your night scene sharply in focus for the whole scene.

To shoot a night scene

1   Zoom in on your subject as tight as you can, viewing it through the LCD viewer.

2   Change to manual focus and adjust until your centre of interest is in sharp focus.

3   Zoom out from your subject, and then frame the scene using either the LCD viewer or the camcorder eyepiece.

4   Shoot the scene.

Once you've established the correct focus for your scene, don't be tempted to zoom in or out again—you'll lose focus if you do.

Exposure

The term exposure refers to the amount of light allowed through the camcorder lens. Getting this right often poses problems: too much light and the shot is over exposed; too little and it's under exposed.

Most camcorders have automatic exposure, which adjusts automatically according to the filming conditions. However, there will be times when you will need to adjust the exposure manually.

For example, filming a subject in heavy shade (under trees for example) commonly causes exposure problems. In this case, the camcorder's automatic exposure adjusts to allow for the average lighting and this means that the detail of the subject is lost.

Use the following technique to ensure that the subject of your shot is correctly exposed.

To shoot in shade

1 Zoom in on your subject as tight as you can, viewing it through the LCD viewer.

2 Change to manual exposure.

3 Adjust the exposure until you have achieved the desired level of lighting.

4 Zoom out from the subject, and then frame the scene using either the LCD viewer or the camcorder eyepiece.

5 Shoot the scene.

Lux

The measurement of actual light available at a given distance, in any situation, is measured in units called 'lux' (symbolized lx). Your camcorder will have various settings to determine how much light it allows to enter the lens (usually by adjusting exposure and/or shutter speed). Experiment with these settings to see their effects on a shot.

Stock library

There are a couple of reasons you should shoot more raw footage than you think you need for a particular project.

To begin with, you'll have more material to work with during the editing phase.

Secondly, you can build up a library of stock shots that you can use in other projects.

Building your stock library

Particularly useful are non-specific shots that you can use in any video—sunsets, landscapes, seascapes, and so on. Such shots are great for transitions, or to 'set the scene.'

Audio Recording

It may surprise you to know that the audio track of a film production is more important than the video track. However, if you think about it, this does make sense—it's much more difficult to watch a television with distorted sound than one with a distorted picture.

🎙 **Built-in or external microphone?**

When shooting your movies, your goal is to capture good video footage and clear soundtracks. To do this, you need to get the microphone as far away as possible from the camcorder (so that you don't record the sound of its motor) and as close as possible to the subject. Obviously, if you're using a built-in microphone, this is difficult to achieve!

Most built-in microphones are of poor quality, so to get the best results, it's worth investing in a good quality external microphone. You'll find this especially valuable to capture audio when your subject is some distance from the camera, or when there is unwanted noise in the location where you are shooting.

Microphone types

When buying a microphone, there are many types and sizes to choose from. Generally, the longer the microphone, the more sensitive it is in one direction. Shorter microphones tend to pick up sound from all around.

As well as **built-in** (on-camera) microphones, which pick up sound from all directions, you can buy:

Hand-held microphones—these plug into the camera, automatically disconnecting the built-in microphone. These microphones pick up sound very close to them; they can also be placed on a table or floor stand. Hand-held microphones are classed as **dynamic** microphones.

In general, your video and audio tracks should speak for themselves. However, there are times when you might want to add narration. In these cases, you should write a script before you begin recording. While your script does not have to be word-for-word, it should outline all the content that is to be included. Avoid stating the obvious.

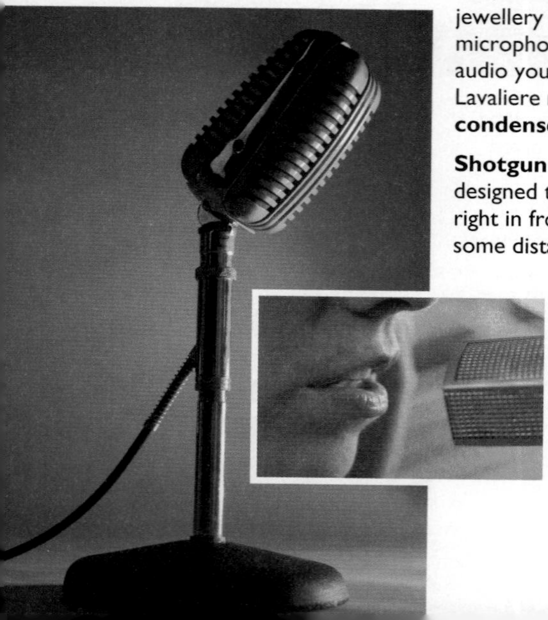

Lavaliere (wireless) microphones—these are attached to a battery pack, which the speaker can put in a pocket or attach to a piece of clothing. Lavaliere microphones are especially good for recording the sound of a speaker who is moving around. If you use one, be aware that long hair and jewellery can rub against the microphone and interfere with the audio you are trying to record. Lavaliere microphones are **condenser** microphones.

Shotgun microphones—these are designed to capture sounds that are right in front of you, and generally some distance away.

While the range of shotgun microphones varies, they tend to be predominantly **condenser** type.

As this section shows, all microphones are essentially one of two main types: dynamic or condenser.

Dynamic mics

Dynamic microphones operate on an electromagnet principle, using a wire coil and magnet to create the audio signal. These microphones are versatile and ideal for general-purpose use. Relatively sturdy and resilient, they are better suited to handling high volume levels, such as from certain musical instruments or amplifiers. Dynamic microphones do not require batteries or external power because they react to vibrations of sound.

Condenser mics

Condenser microphones are more common in camcorder recording equipment and use a capacitor (a permanent battery) to convert acoustical energy into electrical energy.

Condenser microphones require power from a battery or external source to charge the capacitor.

The resulting audio signal is stronger than that from a dynamic microphone. Condensers are generally more sensitive and responsive, so they are ideal for capturing more subtle audio tracks but less suited to high-volume or close interview work.

There are three types of condenser microphones to choose from:

Electret condenser microphones are the cheapest and most commonly available. Their advantage is that they derive their power directly from the camcorder. However, in damp conditions they have a tendency to be noisy.

AF condenser microphones are also susceptible to problems caused by humidity. In addition, they also require a power supply. These microphones are therefore highly unsuitable for outdoor work.

RF condenser microphones are more complex and slightly more fragile. However, because they are not affected by humidity RF microphones are the preferred choice for recording audio outside.

Before you decide which microphone is best suited to your needs, however, you also need to consider microphone **directionality**.

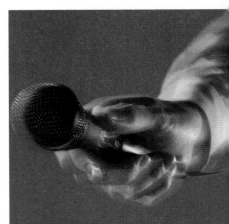

Directionality

A microphone's directionality refers to its sensitivity to sound from various directions. Some microphones pick up sound equally from all directions, others pick up sound only from one direction or a particular combination of directions. The types of directionality are divided into the following main categories: **omnidirectional**, **unidirectional**, and **superdirectional**.

Omnidirectional

Also known as **nondirectional** microphones, these record sound from all directions and are generally used for interview work and for capturing general audio from an event. Because they pick up surrounding noise, however, they must be kept close to the subject when doing interview work. (Built-in microphones are omni-directional.)

Although useful in the right situation, picking up sound from every direction is not usually a good idea because the resulting audio tends to be quite unfocused. If you want to capture sound from a particular subject it is likely to be overwhelmed by other noise.

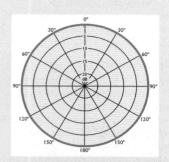

Omnidirectional

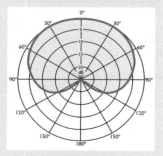

Unidirectional

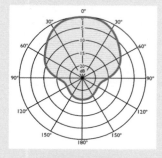

Superdirectional

Unidirectional

Also known as **cardioid** microphones, these pick up sound in a heart shape area, mainly from the direction in which they are pointed. These microphones are used when you want to limit unwanted noise. They are good general purpose microphones.

Superdirectional

Also known as **hypercardioid** or **gun** microphones, these are very directional microphones, making them ideal for isolating the sound from a subject or direction when there is a lot of ambient noise.

These microphones are also good for recording distant sounds, for example, chirping birds.

Audio tips and tricks

Once you've chosen the right microphone for your needs, the following tips will help you get the most out of your audio recordings.

- Test your equipment before you leave. It's better to find out a microphone isn't working when you're at home than on location.

- Take a pair of earphones with you so you can listen to the sounds you're capturing.

- If you're using a built-in microphone, to get the clearest possible audio and reduce unwanted background noise, get as close as possible to your subject (about three feet away is best if you want to get a good head and shoulders shot). Don't forget that the microphone will also capture any noise you make.

- If using an external microphone, position it away from the camera and as close to the subject as possible (approximately six inches away from a person's mouth is optimum). Make sure you place it on a stable surface where it won't move.

- Before you start recording, eliminate any unnecessary background noise. If you don't, you're likely to get different background sound with each shot.

- Record some background noise to add to your audio tracks. During editing, you can then use these tracks to create continuity between shots.

- In windy conditions, shield the microphone as much as possible. Use a windshield on the microphone; if you don't have one, you can use a large umbrella or try covering the microphone with a cloth.

- Be aware of the impact of music and sound effects on your video footage. Choose carefully to reflect the feeling and pace of your shots.

- When recording live music events, make sure you record the entire piece of music. During the editing phase, you can then select your best video shots and lay them against this continuous soundtrack.

- Do a trial run to identify any distortion and determine consistent sound levels from your subjects and background sources. Do a test, then play it back on your earphones.

- To reduce ambient noise when recording narration, be sure to close the doors and windows to the room you are in. To reduce noise further, record in a corner of the room, in an area that is 'insulated' with absorbent material of some kind (you can use foam, blankets, curtains, carpet, mattresses, even egg boxes!).

- To reduce popping sounds in recorded speech, particularly in the pronunciation of aspirated plosives (such as the first 'p' in 'popping'), use a **pop filter** (also known as pop screen)—a small screen placed between the microphone and the speaker.

  Commercially available pop filters vary in price, but all typically consist of nylon or metal mesh stretched over a circular frame. If you're on a tight budget, you can make your own by stretching nylon tights or stockings over a wood, plastic or metal loop—you could use an embroidery hoop, a kitchen sieve, or a bent wire coat hanger.

Editing

Even if you have bought the best equipment and captured some great video and audio footage, all your efforts will be wasted if you make the wrong editing decisions.

The video editing process is very similar to putting together any type of presentation—the editor 'cuts and pastes' various video and audio segments together, and adds effects and titles where necessary.

Home computer video editing tools like MoviePlus produce results that were previously attainable only in production houses—and because you can preview and adjust each edit decision, this environment gives you exceptional freedom. Before you begin, ensure that your computer meets the recommended requirements for the hardware and software you're using.

Video editing requires both artistic and technical skills. It also requires a lot of time—and this applies to both the novice and professional editor.

> You should consider the editing phase even as you're filming your video. This will help you to make the right decisions about what to shoot, and where and how to shoot it. Aim to film each shot from more than one angle. This will give you plenty of options when you come to edit your movie.

The artistic process involves deciding what elements to keep, delete, or combine so that they come together in a coherent and visually pleasing manner.

The technical process consists of knowing how to use MoviePlus to achieve your artistic goals.

In this section we'll set you on the right track and help you achieve results you can be proud of.

Take tips from the pros

There's nothing wrong with taking inspiration from professional productions. Notice how establishing shots are used, what transitions are most effective, and how clips are put together—sometimes so seamlessly that you hardly notice, and at other times quite dramatically.

Keep it short

Audiences have a limited attention span. To hold their interest, keep your production 'tight.' It only takes a few seconds for the viewer to absorb and understand a static shot so these clips should be short.

Longer clips should be long enough to depict all the action, but generally should not continue beyond this point.

Keep it moving

Good video needs action. MoviePlus makes it easy for you to cut out the boring bits (the extra two minutes it takes your child to open each of his Christmas presents, for example), leaving just the footage you want to use.

Tell a story

When assembling your video clips, your goal is to build them into a coherent story or sequence of events.

A common method is to start with an establishing shot to set the scene, and then move on to the action scenes. The clips should be ordered logically and should build towards a climax. Ideally, try to cut different size shots together. For example, when cutting together several shots of the same person, vary the size of the shot as well as the camera angle.

Think about pace and style

When you planned and shot your video, you will also have thought about how you wanted your finished production to look. The pace and style of your video will be affected not only by the visual and audio content, but on the length of your shots and the way in which you move from one clip to the next.

💡 If your captured footage is very big, you might prefer to do some editing before you import into MoviePlus. (You may also run out of disk space if you try to import everything.)

Edit your footage in MoviePlus

If you're working on a small production, the simplest way to edit your movie in MoviePlus is to:

1 Add all your clips to the **Media** pane.

2 Select each of your clips in turn and trim any unwanted pieces.

3 Drag the clips you want to use onto the storyboard, in the sequence your prefer.

(For instructions on how to do this, see the **How To** pane.)

Don't overdo transition effects

A transition is the process of changing from one shot to the next.

Professional productions generally stick to the more standard transition types and don't jump from one type to another.

Unless you're really comfortable with the editing process, it's best to stick with the smooth and simple cut, dissolve, and fade to black or from black. (For more on transitions, see page 44.)

As you play your video and audio footage, you'll notice some obvious 'natural' cutting points. For example, a person getting up from a chair during a close-up shot, a drink being put down on a table, or even a simple head turn. In audio footage, a cut may occur when an sound is heard off-camera—a doorbell ringing, a person laughing, a car engine starting up, and so on.

Make careful cuts

Cuts within a scene should be virtually seamless and the viewer should hardly be aware of them. This is easier said than done. However, you'll find that the more editing you do, the better your cutting technique will become. Cuts appear more natural if they have a purpose, for example, if a cut from one scene to the next provides more information about the story or location (you can use different camera angles to do this). Similarly, switching between two characters involved in a conversation will also appear natural.

Storyboard mode

For simple projects, the storyboard is all you need to quickly create a movie. Simply drag clips, photos, and background music tracks onto the storyboard from the **Media** pane.

You can reorder your clips; trim away unwanted portions; add text, transitions, and special effects; and finally share your finished movie in a variety of popular formats.

The **How To** pane covers the Storyboard mode in detail.

Timeline mode

For more advanced projects, the timeline offers all the manual editing operations that traditional film editors require.

For example, you can work with multiple video and audio tracks; add and edit envelopes; apply masks and overlays, and more.

For detailed information on working in Timeline mode, see online Help. For step-by-step instructions on how to create specific effects, see the tutorials in Chapter 3, "Timeline Techniques."

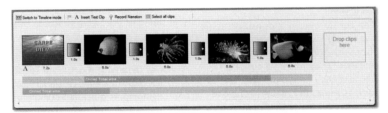

Storyboard mode

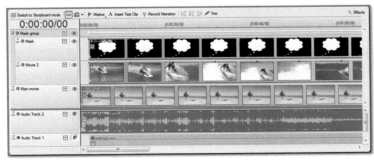

Timeline mode

Transitions

MoviePlus provides a wide selection of transition effects, ranging from simple fades to more complex geometric designs. As a beginner, you may be tempted to use them liberally throughout your project. However, if your aim is to create a professional looking video, avoid temptation and stick to the basics.

Do some research—you'll find that you hardly ever see fancy transitions in movies or television shows.

The following list describes the simplest and most common transition methods used.

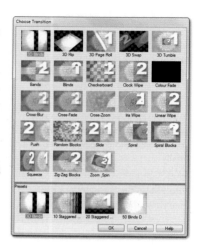

The cut

The cut isn't really a transition at all, but simply involves replacing one shot with another. Cuts are fast and efficient. They maintain continuity because they mimic the way we look at things in real life—our line of vision quickly jumps from one thing to the next. For this reason, cuts are the best way to keep the action rolling at a good pace (so timing is key). Fancier transitions can be distracting and slow down the pace.

The fade

This is when a shot gradually fades to (or from) a single colour, usually black or white. It's a useful (and often used) transition, and in movies typically occurs when the story changes locations.

The speed of the fades indicates the importance of the change in time and/or location between scenes.

A slower fade with more time spent on black indicates a more significant end/beginning. A quick fade to/from black might indicate a time lapse of a few minutes or hours, whereas a long fade indicates a much bigger change.

The wipe

This effect is more obvious than the fade and the viewer is supposed to notice it. The wipe denotes a major change in location or time. It might also be used to show a main character changing over time, wiping between clips of him or her at various points in time.

Effects and image adjustments

It's possible that your clips are similar in term of brightness, colour balance, and so on. It's also likely that you'll want to make some adjustments to correct some images, to give your clips a more consistent appearance, or to add visual interest by applying a creative effect.

In MoviePlus, you can do all of this using the **Effects** gallery.

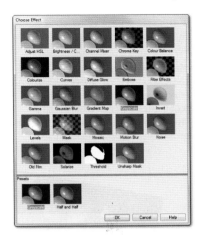

Greyscale effect

For details on working with transitions and effects in MoviePlus, see online Help or the **How To** pane (for Storyboard mode only).

In this section, we've touched on the principle techniques of video editing.

MoviePlus provides you with all the tools you need to create impressive movies, and there are many other techniques you can use to add interest and professionalism to your projects.

For example, you can apply masks and overlays, create split screen and Picture in Picture effects, work with opacity and transforms, and so on.

For more details and step-by-step instructions, see Chapter 3, "Timeline Techniques."

Tips & Tricks

This chapter describes some of the events that you're most likely to want to shoot, and provides general guidelines to help you do so successfully—the first time!

The Wedding Video

Whether you're an experienced filmmaker, or a complete novice, sooner or later you will end up shooting a wedding.

If the bride and groom ask you to film their special day, however, think carefully before agreeing. A wedding is a very special occasion and the purpose of the wedding video is to remind the couple of a wonderful day and the friends and relatives who shared the celebration with them.

If you're new to shooting and editing video, this is a daunting task—if you miss an important shot, you won't get a second chance.

However, when armed with the right equipment and knowledge, it can also be an enjoyable and very rewarding challenge.

This section provides some guidelines and tips to help you produce a wedding video you can be proud of.

Planning

This is an essential step. If you take the time to plan your wedding video and identify your approach, you'll avoid many of the common pitfalls.

Well before the event, meet with the bride and groom and discuss their likes, dislikes, and expectations of a wedding video.

For example:

- Are there any special shots they want you to include.

- Do they want their video to be glamorous, joyful but serious, or can you also include some humorous moments (tasteful, of course).

- How much coverage do they want and what will be considered obtrusive.

- Is there a particular piece of music they'd like you to use as a backing track. If this decision is left up to you, choose something gentle and romantic. Again, avoid humour that might offend.

- Do they want you to add credits to the end of the video; if so, make a note of the names and correct spelling.

Location

Check out the locations where the ceremony and reception are to be held in advance—if possible, at the same time of day you will be shooting the video.

If the ceremony is to be held in church, make sure that you can film inside.

Find the best places to set up the camera(s). Churches are particularly badly lit for shooting video. Watch out for backlighting and look for positions that allow you to shoot away from the windows.

If you're the only person filming, the best place to set up is behind the wedding official on the groom's side.

This will give you the best close-up shots of the bride during the exchange of vows.

If you're working with two cameras, position the second one in the back third of the church, to one side.

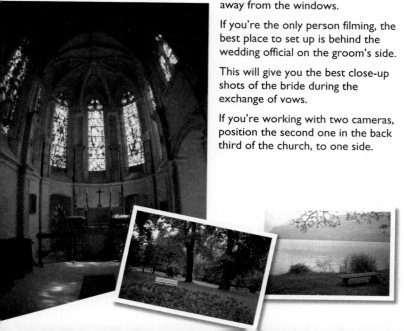

🔌 Shots you must get

Your wedding video won't be complete if it doesn't include these shots:

Before the ceremony

- Bride and bridesmaids getting ready.
- If the locations are close, the groom and best man getting ready.
- Exterior of the church.

At the ceremony

- The groom and best man arriving.
- The guests arriving—especially the parents of the bride and groom.
- The bride and bridesmaids arriving and walking down the aisle.
- If you have a second camera positioned at the back of the church or room, take a shot of the groom watching the bride walk towards him.
- Long shot of the ceremony.
- Pledging of vows and exchange of rings.
- The signing of the register.
- After the ceremony, make sure you leave early enough to capture the couple leaving.
- Confetti being thrown.
- The wedding cars.

At the reception

- Head to the reception in time to shoot the couple arriving.
- All the guests including parents, bridesmaids, pageboys, etc.
- Group shots—follow the official photographer to get these.
- The cake, floral decorations, glasses of champagne, and so on.
- Best man's toast.
- The cutting of the cake.
- The couple's first dance.
- Interviews with the bride and groom—prepare your questions in advance.
- Interviews with guests.
- Cake, presents, decorations, flowers, a wedding invitation, an order of ceremony, or any other interesting and appropriate wedding 'paraphernalia'—these shots can make great transitions and cutaways.
- Keep a look out for any amusing incidents. (See "Shots you shouldn't get," on the next page.)

Wedding rehearsal

Attend it!

In addition to helping you get to know the layout of the location, it will also allow you to get some shots that might be difficult to shoot on the day itself.

For example, a close-up of the rings being exchanged. You might even want to include pre-wedding 'interviews' with the bride and groom.

Teamwork

Discuss your plans with the photographer to make sure you won't be in the way. You should do this before the wedding day, but if you can't, make sure you do it early in the day before you start shooting.

If you need help setting up equipment, arrange this well in advance—don't assume that you'll find a volunteer on the day. If you're recruiting someone to operate a second camera, make sure he or she understands your ideas about camera motion, effects, pan and tilt, and so on.

 Shots you shouldn't get

No matter how funny you think they look, don't film people who have had too much to drink.

You should also avoid taking shots of people eating, backs of heads at the ceremony, and people backlit by windows.

Equipment

Consider using a tripod. It will be a long day and it can be tiring to hold the camcorder steady for long periods of time. It's also very difficult to do and you don't want shaky footage of the big moment!

If you've recently bought new equipment, make sure that:

- It works properly.
- You are comfortable using it before the wedding—this applies to any event you're filming.

On a more serious note, don't leave your equipment unattended.

Even though you're surrounded by friends, you shouldn't assume that your camcorder will be safe if left for a few minutes.

 Be professional

If you want to do a good job of your wedding video, have that one glass of celebratory champagne but otherwise stick to non-alcoholic drinks.

By all means take a couple of shots of the champagne glasses though!

Shooting

The big day has arrived. It's a happy event, but keep in mind that it can also be a stressful time for some, especially the bride. Be as considerate and inconspicuous as you can. You'll want to get close-up shots, but don't be intrusive.

To capture the entire event, there will be times when you'll have to zoom. Do it slowly and avoid constantly zooming in and out. Do make use of your zoom, however, to frame a shot before shooting.

Remember that the bride is the star of the day, but don't forget the groom!

As well as being a romantic event, a wedding is also a fun time, and a time for family and friends to get together. You want your video to portray this, so be sure to capture interactions between guests, friends chatting, children playing, and so on.

Have fun yourself—if you're well-prepared, this should be possible!

You will no doubt have to think on your feet and improvise, but do the best you can.

Most importantly, shoot lots of footage.

Don't worry about the boring bits—you can edit them out later!

Editing

Don't rush the editing process. It's a good idea to watch the entire footage several times before even starting to edit it.

MoviePlus provides a wide range of effects and transitions. For a wedding video, however, we strongly suggest that you keep it simple. Stick to simple transitions—straight cuts, fades, and dissolves. By doing this, you'll create a movie that will age gracefully and that you won't be embarrassed to watch in years to come.

If you want to use something special like a heart-shaped transition or mask, don't overdo it. Pick just one or two special frames. This will create much more visual impact.

While the couple might be happy to sit down and watch hours of footage, their friends and family probably won't!

For best results, keep the final edited video short (aim for under 60 minutes). Many couples will want you to include the full ceremony, but you should check this with them first.

Keep the original footage, but let the happy couple see your edited version before they see the long version.

> While we don't recommend you overdo the special effects in any video production, some effects can add a romantic feel to a wedding video. For example, MoviePlus's Diffuse Glow effect broadens highlights to create a gentle, soft focus effect.

Our first dance...

◉ Break it up

Wedding videos can be quite long. To maintain the interest of your audience, it's important to break the footage up into sections. You can do this in several ways:

- Make use of cutaways to lead the audience out of one section of the video and into another.

- Create visual interest by including shots of the same scene taken from different positions or using different camera angles.

- Use titles to divide sections of the video—the church, the reception, the bestman's toast, etc. If done properly, these can add a stylish and professional-looking element to your video production.

- MoviePlus lets you work with text in a variety of different ways to create interesting and effective title sequences.

Presentation

Presentation is very important. You've spent time and energy creating your wedding video. Don't spoil it by presenting it to the couple on a generic DVD with their names scrawled in marker pen!

Create a special DVD or VCD cover. It doesn't have to be elaborate, a simple graphic design or shot of the couple will do just fine. It will add an air of professionalism to your project, and the bride and groom will appreciate this final touch.

For a really professional look, buy 'printable' VCDs and DVDs and print your design directly onto the surface.

We hope you've found the tips in this section useful, and are feeling more confident about shooting and editing your next wedding video.

The Christmas Video

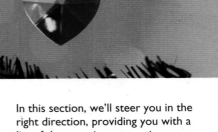

Everyone who owns a camcorder creates a video of the family at Christmas. If you're new to filmmaking, this can be a excellent opportunity to practice your skills and techniques—there are lots of great moments to capture, your subjects are happy and relaxed, and if you are at home you are very familiar with the location!

In comparison to the wedding video then, the Christmas video is a relatively simple and stress-free project. However, you still want to produce a film that entertains your audience and maintains their interest. This means that while you don't have to storyboard your project, you do need to stick to some basic rules.

In this section, we'll steer you in the right direction, providing you with a list of the most important tips to help you create a Christmas video you can be proud of—and your family will want to watch.

Planning

Start early. There are lots of things you can do in preparation for the big day:

- Make sure you are comfortable with your **equipment** (of course, you won't be able to do this if your camcorder is a Christmas gift!).

- Make a list of the **main shots** you want to include, and then think about how you can vary angles and shot types to make them more interesting.

- Take some **practice footage** to help you decide on the best place(s) to set up the camcorder. Pay particular attention to backgrounds and lighting.

- Find some appropriate music for your **backing track**. For example, is there a song that has particular meaning for the family? You might also want to ask family members for their suggestions.

- Don't wait until Christmas Day to start filming. You can get some interesting footage of the **preparations** too—the pudding being stirred, the cake being iced, presents being wrapped.

Shooting

Christmas Day has arrived and you're all ready to shoot.

Obviously you're going to want to capture the main 'action.' However, you should also look out for appropriate shots to use as cutaways—presents under the tree, close-ups of decorations and lights, the turkey, and so on.

During the editing phase, you can use these shots to transition between scenes. If used effectively they can really give your project a professional touch.

In addition to the loud and boisterous shots of the kids opening their presents, include some quiet moments (you'll probably have to wait until later in the day.)

And don't forget the adults—yourself included! Capture interactions between family members, gifts being exchanged, and so on. Take some time off and move to the other side of the lens. Show someone how to use the camcorder and get them to take some shots of you.

If you're lucky enough to have a white Christmas, go outside for a while. Get the family to build a snowman together, or take that new sled for a test run...

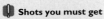

Shots you must get

- The kids helping with the Christmas baking.
- Presents being wrapped.
- The Christmas tree and decorations being put up.
- Christmas lights in the neighbourhood.
- The kids putting out mince pies and a glass of sherry for Santa, and a carrot for Rudolph (don't forget to take a couple of bites before morning!).
- Christmas morning and present unwrapping.

  You don't need to capture every single present, but make sure you film enough. You can always edit out the boring bits.

- Family members arriving for Christmas dinner.
- The family around the table when the turkey is brought in.
- The children playing with their favourite gifts.
- The Queen's Speech—ok, maybe not all of it! But shoot it all and then you can choose which bits to keep during the editing phase.

Mix it up

If you're not careful, all your Christmas videos will look the same (they'll also look similar to everyone else's!).

To avoid this, try to use a different technique each time. For example, create an 'old-fashioned family Christmas' by applying a sepia tone, or experiment with different focus effects.

Editing

If your first 'family Christmas' video is a success, then you'll probably want to capture the celebrations year after year. The problem with this is that if you adopt the same approach each time, you'll end up with a collection of videos that all look very similar.

There are many things you can do to add a different look and feel to your project.

While shooting, you can experiment with unusual camera angles and different shot types to add variety to your movie.

However, the editing phase offers you even more flexibility and the opportunity to get really creative.

Once you've added your video and audio tracks to the MoviePlus storyboard or timeline, there are a multitude of different techniques and effects at your disposal.

For example, you can:

- Experiment with transition effects.

- Apply a greyscale effect to create a black and white movie.

- Create an 'old-fashioned family Christmas' feel with a 'Sepia' or 'Victorian' tone.

- Apply different focus and filter effects.

- Adjust levels and colour balance.

- Apply masks and overlays.

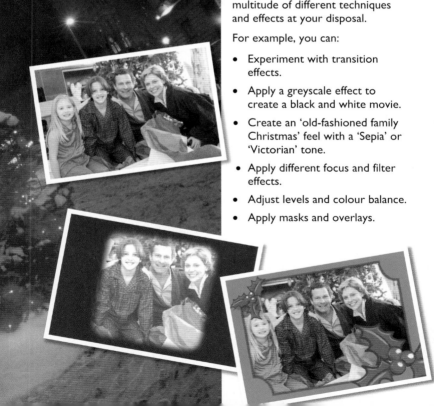

The Party Video

A child's birthday party is an exciting and fun event—one that parents and child will want to remember for years to come. In fact, it's a perfect excuse to get out your camcorder and capture those special moments on video!

Because of the light-hearted nature of children's parties, you can really get creative and employ some shooting and editing techniques that you would not normally use in other projects.

In this section, we'll provide you with tips to help the shoot go as smoothly as possible. We'll also give you some editing ideas to help you create interesting effects that will really make a difference.

Planning

If you're a parent, you'll already know that children's parties are very busy! To avoid ending up with haphazard footage that will be difficult to edit, you must be organized.

Use the following guidelines to help you plan for this project:

- As usual, pay attention to lighting, framing, backgrounds, and so on.

- If you have new equipment, make sure you're comfortable using it well before the day of the party.

- Plan your shots ahead—decide on the best place(s) to shoot from. Remember that the children will be moving (even running!) around, so while you want to capture the action, you don't want to be in the way or cause a tripping hazard.

- Choose some appropriate background music— your child's favourite song, or one that fits with the party's theme.

- Perhaps the most important tip of all is that you should try to shoot from the children's level rather than from yours.

Shooting

Children's parties are not sedate affairs: there's always lots going on—often in multiple locations. This can often tempt you into 'firehosing'—panning all over the scene in an attempt to capture everything. The resulting footage is extremely irritating because it never focuses on anything.

To avoid this, frame each shot *before* you start to shoot. There may be a lot happening, but you can only focus on one thing at a time so choose wisely.

Keep the camera steady and let your subjects dictate the movement.

When you do move, do it slowly and smoothly. You may be eager to switch to the next scene, but make sure you shoot long enough so that the resulting footage makes sense.

(By the way, it's fine to keep the camera rolling while you move from one shot to the next because you'll trim this section in the editing stage.)

🛎 Shots you must get

- Party preparations, decorations being put up, excited child getting ready for the party.
- Guests arriving.
- The birthday cake, party food, balloons, gifts, etc.
- The birthday girl or boy—lots of footage of the star of the day.
- All the children sitting round the table for the birthday tea.
- Opening cards and gifts.
- Party games and activities—try to vary your shots from one child to another.
- The candles being blown out and the 'Happy Birthday to You' moment.
- Include close-ups of individual faces; medium shots of two or three children interacting; and wide shots of the group.

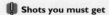

💡 Have fun!

Experiment with different camera angles. Shoot from above (stand on a chair), or try some tilted shots. Unusual shots will break up the standard footage, and make your finished movie much more interesting to watch.

If you're filming alone, it's a good idea to use two video cameras. Set one up on a tripod, or stable surface, in a spot where you'll capture the main 'action.' This leaves you free to focus on close-ups, amusing interactions between the party guests, reaction shots, and so on.

If the entire party is to take place in the same room, you can leave the camera and tripod set up in the same spot.

However, you may need to move it if certain activities take the children into a different location—outside for a treasure hunt, into the dining room for the party tea, and so on.

If you only have one camera, don't try to capture everything in one long shoot. Break it up into a series of shorter 'chunks' that you can put together later in the editing phase.

Include interviews with the birthday boy or girl and the party guests. Think up some fun questions ahead of time:

- What's the best thing about birthday parties?

- What's your favourite party game/food?

- What's the best thing about being 6?

Clips like these make great transitions between other scenes and are guaranteed to entertain your audience.

While the children are busy eating, take advantage of those few minutes to get some good close-ups.

Editing

When it comes to editing your birthday party footage, the possibilities are endless.

With MoviePlus, you have all the flexibility you need to create a really entertaining movie and family keepsake. You'll be filming your child's parties for many years, so it's a good idea to give each project a different look and feel.

Here are a few ideas to get you started:

- Turn your project into a fun music video by adding an appropriate background audio track. (If the children are older, you can even take footage of them lip-synching along to the chorus.)

- Give your movie a cartoon-style feel and add your own amusing commentary by applying 'thought-bubble' overlays to selected shots.

- Experiment with masks, transitions, and effects.

  A split screen effect, for example, is a great way to create visual interest and break up your more standard footage (try using it in your music video too!)

- Start and end your movie with style—begin with a text headline displaying the name of the 'star,' then finish with rolling credits listing the names of all the party guests.

> To see how to create the effects mentioned here and for general help on MoviePlus, see the **How To** pane, online Help, and Chapter 3, "Timeline Techniques."

The Sports Event Video

Sports events contain many characteristics that create great visual impact—action, excitement, drama, and suspense. This makes them natural, but often tricky, subjects for filmmakers.

Professional filmmakers work with a team of experts—usually several cameramen and commentators. You don't have this advantage so be aware of your limitations.

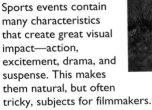

Because of their fast-paced and unpredictable nature, sports events can be difficult to shoot and a certain level of skill and experience is definitely advantageous. If you're a novice filmmaker, therefore, we recommend that you don't make this your first project.

In this section, you'll find tips on planning, shooting, and editing sports events. We hope that they'll help you capture the action and avoid the more common pitfalls.

Planning

It's particularly important that you take the time to plan your project.

- If you're familiar with the sport and players, you'll find it much easier to anticipate the action and position yourself appropriately. Think about the location and the best places to set up your equipment.

- If you're new to the sport, attend a couple of games or events before the shoot to familiarize yourself with the kind of action you'll need to capture.

- Take tips from the pros. Sit down and watch professionally filmed footage of the event you're about to shoot. Make a note of where the cameras are situated, how the action is followed, which camera angles and shot types work best, and so on.

Equipment

Creating a sports event video requires you to keep filming constantly and for a long period of time (a team event, for example, might be 90 minutes long). This can be tiring. We strongly suggest you consider using a tripod—not only to keep you filming through the whole event, but also to help you capture steady shots.

When using a tripod in a public place, you should ask for permission first. Equipment like this can be a hazard so you need to set it up in a place where people are not likely to trip over it.

Check your equipment and charge your batteries (buy spares too) beforehand. There's nothing worse than running out of power part way through a shoot—and you won't be able to go back for an action replay!

> While less steady than a tripod, consider using a monopod (one leg as opposed to three) instead. You'll find it much easier to carry and move around.

Ensure you have enough tape to capture everything. We suggest you change tapes at a convenient time—for example at half time—even if there's still room on the first tape. Use a separate tape to shoot additional footage such as introductory or closing shots.

Shooting

If you can, use two video cameras. Set one up in a position to capture wide-angle footage of the whole event—for a pitch event for example, the best spot is on the centre line. For the second camera, choose a position where you'll be able to capture some interesting shots. In a football match, filming from one of the corners will give you some great shots of goals, as well as reaction shots.

If you are limited to one camera, you should try to position yourself somewhere where you can comfortably capture the whole pitch or arena.

See if other filmmakers are interested in combining efforts. Get each person to film from a different spot and share the footage.

At a football match for example, if you set up on the centre line you'll be able to film the entire pitch but also zoom in on both of the goals.

If you're shooting in a large arena, try to get as far back and as high up as possible so you can shoot over the spectators' heads.

To add variation and visual interest to your movie, use different camera angles—tilting shots, low and high-angle shots, and so on.

In these situations, the rule is to pan, moving the camera gradually and sparingly—a technique that takes practice. (If you can, practise panning and zooming in on different areas before the event begins.)

Another tip is to shoot from a spot where the action will be coming towards you,

When filming a race, for example, start shooting before the event begins and follow the runners as they approach and pass you. Then stop filming and move to a position where you can capture the runners as they cross the finish line.

Don't forget to keep the camera rolling for a few seconds after the race finishes to avoid an abrupt ending.

While it's always advisable to keep zooming to a minimum, this is sometimes inevitable when filming sports events. However, avoid the tendency to zoom quickly from one shot to another. This will result in shaky footage that you won't be able to correct during editing.

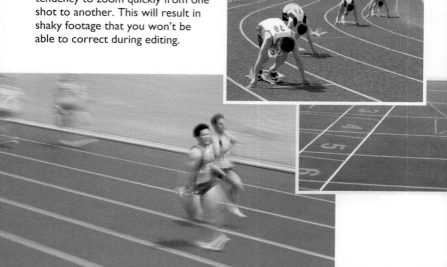

Shots you must get

- Pre-event preparations—the spectators arriving, setting up of equipment, officials getting into position, and so on.

- The players or athletes walking on to the pitch, court, or arena.

- The game or event itself—very important!

- Interesting cutaway shots such as fans cheering when a goal is scored, the referee or other officials, reaction shots of teammates, opponents, and supporters.

- At the end of an event such as a football match, capture footage of the players shaking hands, exchanging shirts, and leaving the pitch. If applicable, include shots of the awards ceremony, close-ups of the winner's trophy or medals.

- If it's a local event, try to get a couple of interviews after the event has finished. Prepare a list of potential questions in advance. (You can even interview some of the fans.)

Remember the **180 degree rule**.

Stay on one side of an imaginary line drawn across the pitch or action, but obtain footage from several different positions.

For example, in a team event, this imaginary line is drawn from one set of goal posts to the other; in an athletic event, it's between the start and finish lines.

By staying on one side of this line, you'll ensure that you are always filming the action in the same direction.

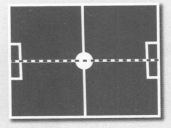

Editing

When editing your footage in MoviePlus, there are lots of effects you can use to give your movie a professional finish.

For example, you can:

- Add overlays and text effects.
- Start your movie with a team line-up or formation.
- Create a picture-in-picture effect.
- Add a score line.

One thing we do suggest, is that you keep transitions to a minimum.

Transitions imply that time has passed between shots. Generally, you'll want to create the impression of continuous action so only use a transition when there is a break in the action (and keep it simple).

> To see how to create the effects mentioned here and for general help on MoviePlus, see the **How To** pane, online Help and Chapter 3, "Timeline Techniques."

The Holiday Video

Family holidays make ideal opportunities for shooting video. Everyone is happy and relaxed and you have the time to experiment with equipment and shooting techniques. In fact, there's really no excuse for making a boring movie!

At some point, we've all been subjected to watching boring footage of a friend's holiday movie. Usually, what makes it boring is the fact that it simply switches from one random scene to the next. In short, it doesn't tell a story.

The aim of your video is to tell the story of your holiday. If you start off by thinking of it in this way, you'll already be on the right track. Every story has a beginning, a middle, and an end. You need to include shots of the preparations for the trip, the events that happen en route, the holiday itself, and the return journey.

In this section, we'll pass on some essential tips and tricks to help you make a holiday movie that everyone will enjoy watching.

Whether you're travelling to some exotic location overseas, or spending your holiday closer to home, here are the basic tips to keep in mind:

- Take your camera everywhere.
- Be sensitive to local people and customs.

- If you plan on spending a lot of time on the beach, we recommend you buy a solid case to protect your camcorder.

- If you have children, film them talking about where they are and what they are doing.

- Most importantly—take *lots* of footage of people. This is what makes a movie interesting. By all means include shots of the local scenery and spectacular views, but make sure that there are people in the shots too (try filming their reaction to the view, for example).

Planning

Ideally, you should plan your holiday video even before you start to pack. You know where you are going and have probably done some research into the places and sights you're likely to visit.

You don't have to create a complex and detailed storyboard, but it's definitely a good idea to sit down and list the main shots you want to include in your 'story.'

 Charge your batteries

If you're vacationing overseas, remember that the voltage is lower so it will take longer to recharge your batteries. Charge them overnight if you can.

Equipment

As with any other project, make sure you have everything you need well in advance. Along with your camcorder, you'll also need extra tapes or memory cards, spare batteries, and a battery charger (don't forget a plug adaptor).

Make a list of your equipment so you don't forget anything when you leave.

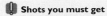 Shots you must get

Here are the shots you shouldn't miss:

- Start by shooting family members packing their suitcases and getting ready to leave. Aim to capture the excitement and anticipation.

- Include shots en route to your destination—the packed car or taxi, airport, the plane at the boarding gate, and so on.

- Capture the family arriving at their destination—checking out the room, the view from the window, etc.

- Capture place names and hotel names.

- Capture the feel of the area by including local architecture, signs, music, food, and (most importantly) people in your shots.

- Look out for sunsets, landscapes, and seascapes. All of these make good cutaways, establishing shots, and title shots.

- Include some shots of passports, plane tickets, a holiday itinerary, a local map, or menu from a favourite restaurant.

- People, people, and more people!

- Include footage of the return journey—children sleeping in the car, sunburned faces, waiting for luggage at the airport, etc.

Shooting

Even though you're on vacation, don't forget that the general rules of filmmaking still apply.

- When framing your shots, use perspective and look for natural frames, and remember the **rule of thirds** (p. 24).

- When shooting, keep in mind the **180 degree rule** (p. 73).

- If you're in a hot and sunny location, pay particular attention to lighting. Avoid backlit shots by shooting with the sun overhead or behind you. If you can't avoid having the sun in the shot, use the camera's 'Backlit' setting.

- The bulk of your holiday footage *must* include people. We can't stress this enough.

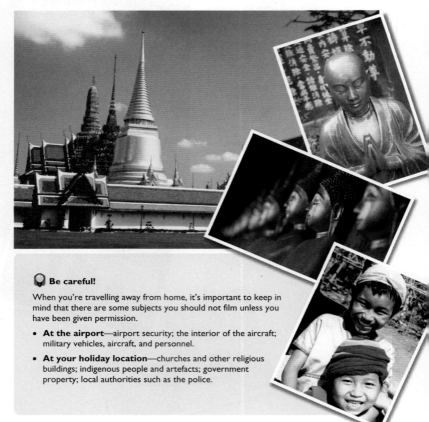

💡 Be careful!

When you're travelling away from home, it's important to keep in mind that there are some subjects you should not film unless you have been given permission.

- **At the airport**—airport security; the interior of the aircraft; military vehicles, aircraft, and personnel.

- **At your holiday location**—churches and other religious buildings; indigenous people and artefacts; government property; local authorities such as the police.

- As always, keep zooming to a minimum. Get as close as possible to your subject instead. If you must zoom, do it slowly and steadily, and hold the shot for a few seconds once you have it framed.

- To capture individual details contained within a particular scene, don't just pan the area. Instead, start by shooting a wide-angle shot to set the scene. You can then move in and capture close-ups of the various details.

- When shooting a panning shot, rather than simply sweeping across the scene, try to follow some action.

  For example, follow a person walking along the beach, a bicyclist riding down the street, or your child walking around the hotel pool.

No one wants to sit through a movie showing endless beach shots, no matter how breathtaking they are.

Film your family and friends swimming, sunbathing, shopping, eating, relaxing, playing sports, sightseeing... This is what will make your movie interesting to watch.

You can include those spectacular beach scenes, but make sure there are people in them—or include them as cutaways or establishing shots to set the scene.

💡 Vary shot types and angles

Your movie will be much more interesting to watch if you include a mixture of shot lengths and angles.

Take the opportunity to experiment by shooting the same shot from a few different angles.

They won't all be successful, but that's what the editing phase is for!

- In addition to shooting movie footage, use your video camera to capture some stills.

  When you return home, you can use these to create a photo slideshow of your holiday.

❗ In MoviePlus Storyboard mode, you can quickly and easily create a movie of your still images, complete with background music, pan and zoom effects, titles and credits, and narration. For details, see the **How To** pane.

Editing

You've had a fantastic holiday and, if you've followed our suggestions, you've captured some wonderful video footage. When the unpacking is done, it's time to sit down and have some fun creating your movie in MoviePlus.

There are lots of techniques and effects you can use to add a professional touch to your project and keep your audience interested in watching it.

- Introduce the various sections of your movie by using establishing shots to set the scene. Begin with a wide-angle shot and then follow it with medium and close-up shots taken from various angles.

- Break up your footage with effective use of cutaways. Close-up shots of local signposts, a map, the menu from your favourite restaurant—even something as simple as a cocktail glass or shells on the beach— all add visual interest and help to tell the story.

- Don't forget to make a slideshow of the still photographs you took!

  With MoviePlus, you can really make your project look professional by adding subtitles, a background audio track, split-screen and picture-in-picture effects, old film effects, and much more. Why not try creating your own 'Ken Burns' effect using pan and zoom functionality.

- For something really different, why not create a 'moving map.'

  This very effective technique is guaranteed to impress, but relatively simple to achieve—add a still image of a map to the MoviePlus timeline, then use pan and zoom to make the map move from location to location as your holiday story unfolds.

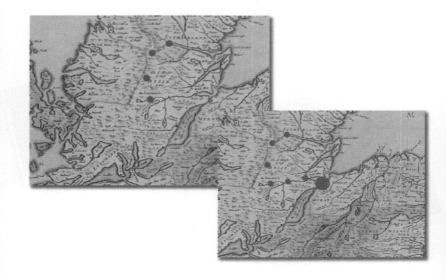

Timeline
Techniques

In this chapter, you'll find a collection of fully-illustrated, step-by-step tutorials designed to help you get the most out of MoviePlus.

These exercises focus on the techniques we think you'll find most useful, and cover a wide range of movie-editing techniques that can be accomplished in Timeline mode.

Techniques covered:

- Trimming and splitting clips
- The transform envelope
- Overlays
- Extending clips
- Fading in and out
- Masks
- Split screen effects
- Picture in Picture
- Audio techniques

Trimming and Splitting

Trimming and splitting are cutting room floor techniques that will tidy up your video clips quickly and easily. Trimming removes unwanted frames from the start or end of a clip; splitting allows you 'cut' a clip into smaller sections, without losing any frames in the process.

In this tutorial, we'll show you how to:

- Trim a clip on the timeline.
- Split a clip into sections.

Trimming

Whatever project you're working on, we suggest that you try to 'shoot everything.' If you follow this advice, you'll have lots of footage to choose from during the editing process. You'll also have footage that you won't want to include in your finished movie.

For example, clips seldom begin or end exactly where you'd like; there may be extra frames at the beginning or end, or you may want to use a short section from the middle of the clip. The solution is to trim the clip—adjusting its in-point and/or out-point to include just the piece you want.

> 🚹 In MoviePlus there are several ways to trim your video clips. The **How To** pane looks at using the **Trim** dialog which can be accessed by clicking the [✎ Trim] button in the **Media** pane or on the context toolbar.

> 🔍 To give yourself more space for the timeline, click **View**, then **Panes** and then click to clear the **How To** check box. This hides the **How To** pane. (Select the check box again to turn it back on.)

Trimming the clip on the timeline

Although there are a number of ways to trim your video clips, we will focus on those specific to the timeline. If you haven't already done so, click [▦ Switch to Timeline mode].

To set the start and end points of a clip

1 Add your video clip to Video Track 1, then zoom into the timeline using the [🔍] **Zoom In** button on the lower Hintline toolbar.

As you zoom in, more thumbnails appear representing the different frames in the clip. (The small marker above the thumbnail shows the exact time the frame will display in the **Video Preview** pane.)

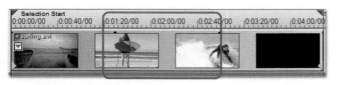

2   Click to select your video clip.

3   Click on the timeline ruler and drag the time indicator to where you
    want your clip to start. You can nudge the time indicator left or right
    by using the keyboard arrow keys.

    The **Video Preview** pane will display the frame at this
    point.

    (If you need to
    be more
    precise, zoom
    into the
    timeline
    further.)

4   On the Timeline
    context toolbar, click
    Set Start Time.
    The start of the clip is
    trimmed to the time
    indicator position.

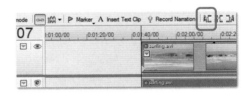

5   Because the clip's duration is shorter, it also takes up less space on the
    timeline. Click and drag the clip to the left to fill in the gap left on the
    timeline.

6   Repeat steps 2 and 3 to select the point where you want your clip to
    end then, on the Timeline context toolbar, click **Set End Time**.
    The end of the clip is trimmed to the indicator position.

    Notice that the audio
    track is trimmed at the
    same time. This is
    because the tracks are
    linked. (For more
    information on linking
    and unlinking clips, see
    online Help.)

> If you have other clips on the timeline, you
> may need to move them to fill in the gaps that
> trimming creates:
>
> • If your clips are **linked**, moving one clip will
>   also move the linked clip.
>
> • You can move linked and unlinked clips (and
>   their associated relationships) at the same
>   time with **Rippling**.
>
> Click **Rippling** on the Timeline context
> toolbar to change the settings.
>
> For details, see online Help.

7   Preview your movie to
    view the results. (You
    might need to press
    to 'rewind' the
    movie first.)

Trimming a clip does not delete any part of the clip itself; instead you can think of it as being hidden. This means that you can revise the trimming—either trim more to make the clip shorter or extend the clip to include more frames—without having to start the process from the beginning each time.

To use the trim cursor to modify a clip

1   Click  **Zoom In** to increase the number of thumbnails displayed on the timeline. This will make it easier for you to be more accurate with your editing. (At the closest zoom, each frame will have its own thumbnail!)

2   Move the cursor over the clip's edge. When the cursor changes to the ⊏╠⇒ **Trim** cursor, click and drag while keeping an eye on the **Video Preview** pane.

You can either drag to make the clip smaller and remove frames, or you can drag in the opposite direction to add frames that were previously trimmed away.

3   Preview your movie to view the results.

> 💡 If you use the time indicator to mark the position of the frame, notice that the edge of the clip snaps to it as the cursor gets near. This handy editing feature is called **snapping**.

Splitting

There will be times where you will want to do something to the frames that are in the middle of a long clip. Perhaps you want to edit out frames that don't work well or remove that shot of the floor! You might also want to create more drama by adding a freeze-frame pause before continuing with the action. This can be achieved by splitting the clip.

Splitting turns one clip into two separate clips, without losing any frames in the process. The clips can then be trimmed or edited separately to achieve the effect that you want.

To split a clip

1   Add your video clip to Video Track 1, then zoom into the timeline using the 🔍 **Zoom In** button on the Hintline toolbar.

2   Click on the Timeline ruler and drag the time indicator to the point where you want to split your clip.

The **Video Preview** pane will display the frame at this point.

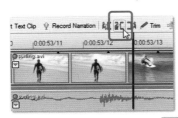

3   Click to select your clip and then click the 🎬 **Split** button on the Timeline context toolbar.

There are now two distinct clips on the timeline, but if you preview your movie, there will be no visible change.

4   You can now trim the new clips individually.

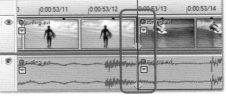

> 🛈 When you split a clip, the linked audio track is also split at the same point.

The Transform Envelope

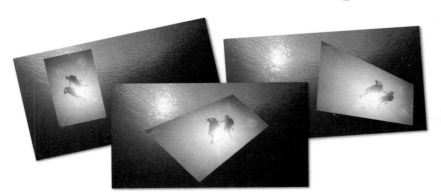

The transform envelope is a key movie editing tool that you'll need to master. For example, the transform envelope allows you to change the size, shape or position of an object, add perspective, and create Picture in Picture and animated effects. It can also be used to adjust the position of the subject in your video or image clips.

In this tutorial, you'll learn how to:

- Change the size and perspective of a graphic.

- Use a preset transform.

- Animate a QuickShape clip using a transform envelope and keyframes.

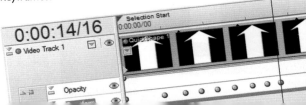

The transform envelope

Although the name may sound rather daunting, the transform envelope is really just a tool that allows you to change the shape, size, rotation and position of a movie or image clip. When used in conjunction with multiple keyframes, the transform envelope enables you to create great looking animation effects. It can also help to 'straighten' wayward footage or zoom in to the subject of your movie.

Sound complicated? Don't worry, it really isn't. If you've ever used image editing or desk top publishing software before, some of the concepts are going to feel quite familiar. Either way, these few examples should get you up and running in no time!

Simple transforms

The transform envelope can be used on an individual clip, or it can be applied at track level. The following example shows you how to change the shape of a QuickShape CG clip. However, the principles are the same whether the clip is a QuickShape, still image or a movie.

To change the size and rotation of a clip in the Video Preview pane

1 Open a new project in timeline mode and then click **Insert > CG clip > QuickShape**.

2 In the **Properties** pane, on the **Properties** tab, change the **QuickShape type** to **Arrow** using the drop-down menu.

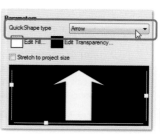

3 On the timeline, on the QuickShape 1 clip, click the 🔽 **Attributes** button and choose **Transform** from the drop-down menu.

4 In the **Video Preview** pane, click and drag on one of the bounding box handles to change the shape and size of the clip.

(If you press the **Shift** key while dragging, you can change the aspect ratio of the clip.)

Try dragging the clip so
that it is bigger than the
preview window (you
may need to zoom out
using 🔍 **Zoom Out**
on the **Video Preview**
pane so that you can
see the clip's bounding
box).

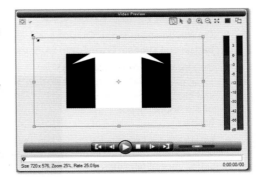

5 Hover the cursor next
to one of the bounding
box handles. When it
changes to the

🖰 **Rotate** cursor, click and drag to rotate the QuickShape.

6 In the **Properties** pane, click **Reset** to undo all of your changes.

To change the size of a clip using the Properties pane

1 On the timeline, on the QuickShape 1 clip, click the 🔽 **Attributes**
button and choose **Transform** from the drop-down menu.

2 In the **Properties** pane, in the **Parameters** section of the
Properties tab, change the **X scale**
and **Y scale** percentage values to
200%. Your QuickShape is now twice
its original size.

3 Change the **X scale** and **Y scale**
percentage values to 50% to make
your QuickShape half of its original
size.

4 Change the **Rotation (degrees)**
value to 45. The
QuickShape is rotated 45
degrees to the left.

5 Change the **Rotation
(degrees)** value to -45 to
rotate the QuickShape 45
degrees to the right.

6 Click **Reset** to undo all of
your changes.

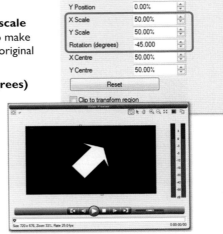

To change the perspective of a clip

1   On the timeline, on the QuickShape 1 clip, click the 🔽 **Attributes** button and choose **Transform** from the drop-down menu.

2   On the **Video Preview** pane, press the **Ctrl** key and click and drag on one of the bounding box handles.

3   Experiment by **Ctrl** dragging the other handles and in various directions.

4   In the **Properties** pane, click **Reset** to undo all of your changes.

To add a preset transform to a clip

1   On the timeline, on the QuickShape 1 clip, click the 🔽 **Attributes** button and choose **Transform** from the drop-down menu.

2   In the **Properties** pane, in the **Transform Envelope** section, click **Gallery...**

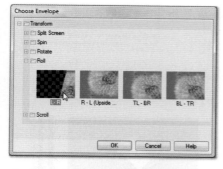

3   In the **Choose Envelope** dialog:

   • Click ⊞ to expand a folder.

   • Hover your cursor over a thumbnail preset to get a 'live' preview of the effect.

   • Choose a preset transform and click **OK**.

4   Preview your in the **Video Preview** pane to see the transform in action.

Transform and keyframes

By combining a transform with keyframes you can create various animated effects, or simply change the position of an object at a set period in time.

To animate a clip using transform and keyframes

1　Open a new project then click **Insert > CG clip > QuickShape**.

2　In the **Properties** pane, on the **Properties** tab, change the **QuickShape type** to **Arrow** using the drop-down menu.

3　On the timeline, click and drag on the end of the QuickShape clip to extend the duration to approximately 30 seconds.

4　On the QuickShape 1 clip, click the ☒ **Attributes** button and choose **Transform** from the drop-down menu.

5　Resize the timeline by dragging its borders. Drag the audio track down to make it smaller and to make the transform envelope visible.

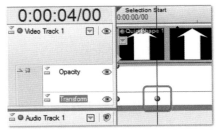

6　Click and drag on the timeline ruler to set the time indicator to approximately 4 seconds, and then click on the transform envelope strip to add a keyframe. (The keyframe snaps into position.)

7　In the **Video Preview** pane, drag the top left corner handle of the bounding box to make the arrow smaller.

8　Click ◀ to return to the start and preview your movie to see the effect.

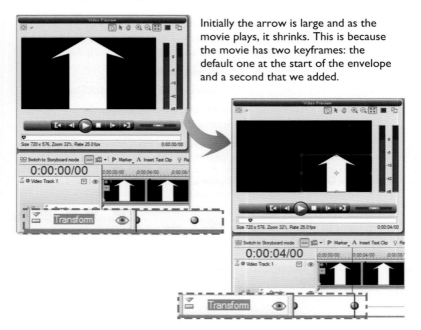

Initially the arrow is large and as the movie plays, it shrinks. This is because the movie has two keyframes: the default one at the start of the envelope and a second that we added.

9   Add more keyframes on the envelope. Remember to drag the time indicator into position and then click on the envelope strip to add a keyframe. On each new keyframe, change the position or size of the arrow.

10 Preview your movie in the **Video Preview** pane to see the effect.

> If you make a mistake and want to remove a keyframe, click to select it and then press the **Delete** key. To delete all of the keyframes at once, click on the Transform header and press the **Delete** key. **Warning**: this will remove **all** the keyframes on the clip.

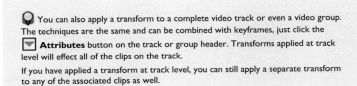

You can also apply a transform to a complete video track or even a video group. The techniques are the same and can be combined with keyframes, just click the **Attributes** button on the track or group header. Transforms applied at track level will effect all of the clips on the track.

If you have applied a transform at track level, you can still apply a separate transform to any of the associated clips as well.

You should now have a short clip of an arrow doing a merry dance around your preview screen. Although this might not be quite the effect that you'll want for all of your movies, it has given you the knowledge you need to put the transform envelope to good use. You can use transforms to create split screen effects, Picture in Picture (PiP), fade your movie into the distance as it ends, or even straighten that lopsided horizon on your favourite home movie.

When combined with other editing techniques (and a little bit of imagination), the possibilities are endless!

If you create a transform that you really like you can save it for later use:

1 On the timeline, select the transform envelope that you want to save.

2 In the **Properties** pane, click **Add to Gallery**.

3 Type a new name for your transform and click **OK**.

The custom transform envelope will now be listed with the other presets in the **Gallery**.

For tips on creating the Split Screen and Picture in Picture effects, see the other tutorials in this chapter.

Overlays

The MoviePlus timeline allows you to create multiple 'layers' of clips, text and graphics—known as overlays. Overlays have a range of applications in movie editing. They can be used to create decorative surrounds, watermarks and signatures, and are often used to display information, especially for sporting events. Graphic overlays can also add interest to slide shows and enhance other video techniques.

In this tutorial, you'll learn how to:

- Add a preset overlay to a clip.
- Create a watermark using text objects.
- Create a scoreboard display using a graphic overlay and text.

Overlays

As a general rule, overlays in movie editing allow part of the underlying track to be visible. This means that they must have transparent sections, reduced opacity or be much smaller in size than the underlying clip. Overlays essentially fall into two categories—

> ⓘ This tutorial assumes that you know how to add media and tracks to your timeline. If you are unsure about how to do this, see the online Help.

text based or graphical (the graphic overlay can be an image or video clip).

Graphic overlays

Graphic overlays are usually images with transparent sections that allow the video clip beneath to show through. You'll find a variety of preset overlays for you to use in your projects in the **Media** pane, in the **Library** tab's **Samples** folder.

To add a graphic overlay

1 Add your video and/or image clips to Video Track 1.

2 Click on Video Track 1 to highlight it and go to **Insert > Video Track**. A new video track is inserted above Video Track 1.

3 In the **Properties** pane, click the **Properties** tab and type the new name 'Overlays' in the **Video Track** text box. Press the **Enter** key. Your track is renamed.

4 In the **Media** pane, click the **Library** tab to display it. If you need to, click ⊞ to expand the **Tutorials workspace** folder and then the **Overlays** folder.

5 Drag the **Silver Full Overlay - WS.png** thumbnail to your Overlays track.

6 Depending on your project settings, the overlay may not completely fit the clip. If this is the case, to resize the overlay, experiment with the ⬚Fit options on the Context toolbar. (In this example, we used **Stretch** from the drop-down list.)

💡 Overlay clips behave just like any other clip in MoviePlus. This means that you can apply transforms, effects and transitions to the clip. For more information, see online Help.

7 By default, the overlay clip will be displayed for 5 seconds. To change the duration, select the 'Silver Full Overlay - WS' clip on the timeline, then, in the **Properties** pane, on the **Properties** tab, type in the new duration for the clip.

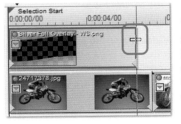

- or -

On the timeline, click to select the clip. Hover over the edge of the clip until the cursor changes to the ⤢ **Trim** cursor. Drag the edge of the clip to the right to extend the duration.

8 Preview your movie to see the overlay in action.

Watermarks

A watermark is text or a small logo that is displayed during part or all of the movie. Watermarks are commonly used by television broadcasters to display the name of the channel, but they can also be used to add the company name, date of creation, advertise website URLs, or as a personal signature by the movie creator.

> 💡 For more information on text formatting, see the **How To** pane or online Help.
>
> Although the **How To** pane content is primarily Storyboard based, text formatting works the same in both workspaces.

To create a watermark

1 On the timeline, select the uppermost track and click **Insert > Video Track**. A new video track will be inserted at the top of the stack.

2 In the **Properties** pane, click the **Properties** tab and type 'Watermark' in the **Video Track** text box. Press the **Enter** key to rename the track.

3 Ensure that the time indicator is at the beginning of the timeline and with the Watermark track still selected, click [A Insert Text Clip] to add a new text clip.

4 In the **Video Preview** pane type in the text that you want to use for your watermark—we used 'mXtv' for 'Motocross TV'—then, click in the **Video Preview** pane, away from the text to deselect it. You'll see a bounding box around the text object.

5 In the **Properties** pane, click the **Format** tab and choose a suitable font from the drop-down list.

6 In the **Video Preview** pane:

- Drag the handles of the bounding box to change the size and shape of your text.

  - Rotate the object by hovering your mouse pointer next to one of the corner handles, and then clicking and dragging the bounding box.

  - Reposition the text object by dragging it to the desired location.

7 In the **Properties** pane, click the **Properties** tab. Change the text **Opacity** to 40%.

8 With your text clip still selected, on the timeline, drag the clip's border so that it extends to the end of the movie.

9 Preview the movie to see your watermark in place.

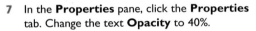

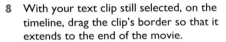

You can set the end time of multiple clips in one go. On the timeline, drag the time indicator to the point where you want the clips to end. Select the clips by holding down the **Ctrl** key as you click. When all of your clips are selected, click 🖫 **Set End Time** on the Context toolbar.

Combining overlays

You can combine overlays to achieve various effects. When working with
multiple tracks and overlays, the order in which they are stacked is critical.
Usually your main footage is at (or near) the bottom of the stack; a
watermark should be placed at the top of the stack. All other overlay
tracks will lie somewhere in between the two.

The following example summarizes how we added a scoreboard to our
motocross movie.

Example: The scoreboard display

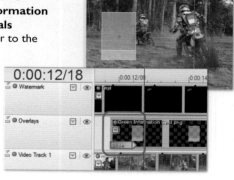

1 We dragged the **Green Information
Card.png** from the **Tutorials
workspace\Overlays** folder to the
Overlays track and used
the **Transform envelope**
to position the card to the
left of the background clip.
We also added a Slide
transition to the Green
Information Card clip.

2 To add the scoreboard text, we inserted a
new track and renamed it 'Overlay text'.
We added a text clip and resized it to fit
the scoreboard. We added extra text
objects to the clip (using $\boxed{A_+ \text{ Add more text}}$ on the
Video Preview pane) and applied
formatting.

ℹ️ You can create your own graphical overlays by using image editing software such as Serif PhotoPlus. All you need to do is create an image that has some transparent areas and save it to a 24 or 32-bit PNG format (with transparency). You can then add it to your MoviePlus project via the **Add Media** button on the **Media** pane.

Using similar techniques, you could also add a title to your movie by combining a graphic overlay with a text clip. Remember that the text track must be above the overlay track if you want the text to appear on top.

Extending Clips

At some point you're bound to want to freeze the action, or even loop a sequence, to create some dramatic effects during your movies. Freeze-frames are also a great way to add a background to credit and title text. This is quick and easy to do with MoviePlus and we'll show you how in the next few pages.

In this tutorial, you'll learn how to:

- Extend a video clip using freeze-frames.
- Loop an audio clip.

Extending clips

In MoviePlus there are two ways to extend clips: by adding freeze-frames (static extensions), and by looping. Freeze-frames can be used as a background to title or credit text at the start or end of a movie, during a zoom to give the subject emphasis, or to give time for transitions between scenes.

You may also need to use freeze-frames to achieve some special editing effects—to allow you to freeze the action while overlaying a cool special effect, or to make time for drama-intensifying narration, for example.

Looping is most useful for extending short audio clips but the technique can also be applied to video. As its name suggests, enabling looping causes the clip to be repeated over and over.

To add a freeze-frame to the end of a clip

1   Add your video clip to Video Track 1 and use the scroll bar to scroll to the end of the clip.

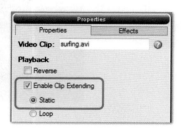

2   With the clip still selected, in the **Properties** pane, on the **Properties** tab, select the **Enable Clip Extending** check box and the **Static** option.

3   On the timeline, hover over the edge of the clip. When you see the ⊕⇒ **Extend clip** cursor, click and drag the edge of the clip to the right.

This extends the clip by freezing the final frame for the duration that you set by the drag operation.

4   Preview your clip in the **Video Preview** pane to see the effect in action. (Click 🔙 to 'rewind' the movie to the start.)

To add a freeze-frame to the start of a clip

1   On the timeline ruler, drag to set the time indicator to approximately 12 seconds.

2   On the timeline, click and drag your clip to the right, so that the edge of the clip is in line with the time indicator.

3   In the **Properties** pane, on the **Properties** tab, select the **Enable Clip Extending** check box and select the **Static** option.

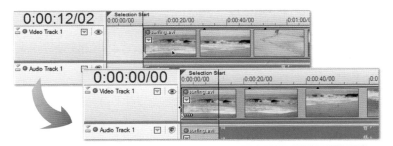

4   On the timeline, hover over the edge of the clip. When you see the $^+_{\square\square}>$ **Extend clip** cursor, click and drag the edge of the clip to the left, so that it starts at 0:00:00/00.

This freezes the first frame of the clip for a duration of 12 seconds.

5   Preview your clip from the start in the **Video Preview** pane to see the effect in action.

As your clip is extended, you will see a small yellow marker (under the clip). This marker shows the original start or end point of your clip, before your static extension was applied.

The black markers along the top of the clip indicate the position of the thumbnail previews. As the clip grows or shrinks on the timeline, the thumbnails will change as they show different frames within the clip.

To add a freeze-frame effect to the middle of a scene, first split the clip into two using ![Split icon] **Split** on the Context toolbar. Drag the right-hand clip to the right to add a small gap to the timeline. Click to select the left-hand clip again. In the **Properties** pane, select **Enable Clip Extending** with the **Static** option. On the timeline, drag the right edge of the selected clip to the right so that it fills the gap. When you preview your movie, it will appear as though the scene freezes and then restarts where it left off.

You can also extend a clip by looping—repeating a clip over a set amount of time. Looping an audio clip is especially useful when you want a background track to play continues throughout your video or slideshow. This is most effective when used with a clip that will loop seamlessly. The following example uses an audio clip; however, the technique is exactly the same for video clips.

To loop a clip

1 On the timeline, on Audio Track 1, click 🔘 **Mute** to temporarily turn off the video clip's audio.

2 Click ⛏ to minimize the track.

3 Click **Insert > Audio Track**. A new audio track is inserted above Audio Track 1.

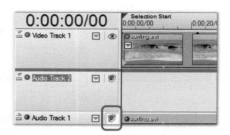

4 In the **Media** pane, click the **Library** tab to display it. Click 🔲 to expand the **Samples** folder, the **Tutorials Workspace** folder and the **Audio** folder.

5 Drag the **Chilled Tribal.wma** thumbnail to Audio Track 2.

🔋 **Looping different file formats**

Seamless looping is not possible with WMA and MP3 audio files as these are not 'gapless' formats—there is always a few milliseconds of blank audio at the end of the file. However, you can always trim the blank audio away in the **Trim** dialog to create a seamless loop.

WAV files are completely 'gapless' and will loop seamlessly without trimming.

6 With the audio clip still selected, in the **Properties** pane, on the **Properties** tab, select the **Enable Clip Extending** check box and select the **Loop** option.

7 On the timeline, hover over the edge of the clip. When you see the ⁺▥⟩ **Extend clip** cursor, click and drag the edge of the clip to the right.

The clip will loop as it is extended on the timeline. The number of loops is shown by the yellow markers displayed beneath the clip; each marker represents one full loop.

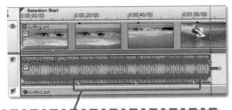

8 Preview the results in the **Video Preview** pane.

█ Trimmed clips

When you select the **Enable Clip Extending** option, trimming a clip on the timeline with the ⊏╪⟩ **Trim** cursor is temporarily disabled. This allows you to extend trimmed clips rather than 'untrimming' them.

> **Stretching clips**
>
> You can also stretch a clip to slow down its playback speed.
>
> **To create a slow motion effect**
>
> 1 Click to select the clip.
>
> 2 Press and hold the **Ctrl** key and drag the right edge of the clip to the right. This makes the clip appear longer on the timeline.
>
> 3 Preview the clip.
>
> If you stretch the clip to double its original length, it will play back at half its original speed.
>
> If you **Ctrl**-drag the right edge of the clip to the left to make it shorter, the action speeds up!

Now that you know how to apply clip extending, there's so much more you can do. Why not try adding another video track so that you can use your freeze-frame image as a background to the movie title or to add interest to the credits?

You can also do more with your audio track, such as panning from left to right or fading the audio in and out. See the "Audio Techniques" tutorial for more information.

Have fun!

Fading In and Out

You're probably already familiar with some of the preset transition effects that you can use to fade your clips in and out, and to blend them into one another. In this tutorial, we'll show you how changing the opacity of a clip gives you greater control and opens up even more possibilities.

You'll learn how to:

- Change the overall opacity of a clip.
- Apply a preset opacity envelope.
- Use keyframes to change the opacity over time.
- Modify an existing opacity envelope.

Fading in and out

Changing the opacity of a clip can create interesting visual effects. For example, it can be used to 'blend' two clips together, create ghostly special effects, and 'soften' graphic or text overlays.

You can set the overall opacity of the clip by changing its properties. However, on the timeline, you can use the **opacity envelope** keyframes. This means that you can change the opacity at a particular frame within the clip, only to change it again moments later.

Opacity effects

To experiment with various opacity settings, you will need at least two video tracks:

- A track with a background image or video clip.

- A track on which to place your 'overlay' clip (this can be a text, QuickShape, movie or image clip).

We will adjust the opacity settings on the upper or 'overlay' track to allow the background track to show through. For our examples, we used an image clip with some transparent sections for the overlay, but any type of clip will do.

To set up your timeline

1 Add your media to the **Media** pane.

2 Click on Video Track 1 to select it, then, in the **Properties** pane, on the **Properties** tab, type 'Background' in the **Video Track** text field. Press the **Enter** key. Your track is renamed 'Background.'

3 Drag your 'background' or main clip onto the Background track.

4 Click **Insert > Video Track**. A new track is inserted above the Background track.

5 In the **Properties** pane, on the **Properties** tab, type 'Overlay track' in the **Video Track** text field. Press the **Enter** key. Your track is renamed 'Overlay track.'

6 Drag your 'overlay' image or video clip to the 'Overlay track.'

If necessary, apply a crop to the clip. (Click 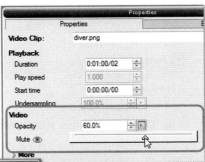 and click **Custom...** in the drop-down list.)

Your overlay clip is displayed in the **Video Preview** pane.

Your timeline is now set up.

To change the overall opacity of a clip

1 Select your overlay clip.

2 In the **Properties** pane, on the **Properties** tab, change the **Opacity** to approximately 60% using the slider.

The effect is updated immediately in the **Video Preview** pane. This helps to fine-tune the effect.

3 Preview your movie.

You will see the background clip showing through the upper, overlay clip, which remains at a constant opacity throughout.

The overall opacity can be set at track level in the same way:

- Click the track header to select the track.

- In the **Properties** pane, in the **Properties** tab, change the **Opacity** value.

If set at track level, the opacity settings are applied to all clips on the track.

Setting the overall opacity in this way will result in a constant level of transparency. However, if we want the opacity to change at different points in our movie, we need to modify the **opacity envelope**. Let's see what happens if we use a preset opacity envelope.

To create an effect using a preset envelope

1 Start a new project and set up your timeline as in the previous steps.

2 On the timeline, on your 'overlay' clip, click the
   ▼ **Attributes** button and click **Opacity** in the drop-down list.

3 On the **Properties** pane, in the **Opacity envelope** section, click ▦Gallery... **Gallery**.

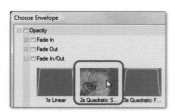

4 In the **Choose Envelope** dialog, click ⊞ to expand the **Fade In/Out** folder. Hover over a thumbnail to see a preview of the effect. Click to select it and then click **OK**. The envelope is applied to your clip.

5 Preview your movie to see the envelope in action.

6 To change the preset to a different one, click ▦Gallery... in the **Properties** tab and select a different preset.

ℹ The ▼ **Attributes** button has four different states. This tells you at a glance whether you already have envelopes or effects applied to the clip, and whether the strips are currently displayed for editing on the timeline. For more information, see the "Timeline Basics" topic in online Help.

Now let's change the opacity at different points in the movie. This is done with keyframes on the opacity envelope.

The first thing we'll do is remove the preset that we added. This is a useful technique to get back to a clean starting point, and works with any type of envelope.

> 🔔 **Keyframes**
>
> In movie editing, keyframes are used to record changes to a video or audio source over time. Each keyframe sets a new starting point for a particular change, such as the application or editing of an effect or envelope.

To remove a preset envelope

1 **Optional:** Click the ▼ **Attributes** button and click **Opacity** in the drop-down list. The envelope is displayed.

2 Click on the envelope header to select the envelope strip and press the **Delete** key.

🔔 This removes **all** changes made to the envelope for that clip, including presets and manual edits.

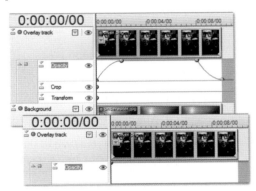

To change opacity using keyframes

1 Zoom into the timeline using 🔍 **Zoom In**. The closer you zoom in, the more accurate you can be with keyframe placement.

By default, the opacity envelope shows a single keyframe. This sets the properties for the entire clip, unless another keyframe is added. Let's do that now.

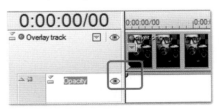

2 Hover the mouse pointer over the first keyframe, click and drag it down.

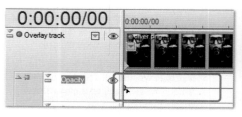

In the **Video Preview** pane, notice that your clip has become more transparent.

On the timeline, the blue line represents the level of opacity over time—at the moment, the opacity stays at a constant level for the duration of the clip.

Let's add a new keyframe.

3 Hover the mouse pointer over the envelope strip until the cursor changes to ✚. Click to add a new keyframe. Drag the keyframe up to the top of the envelope strip. The opacity is increased to 100%.

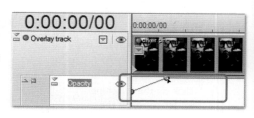

The keyframe is highlighted red to show that it is selected. Notice that the line between the two keyframes is straight. This shows that the type of interpolation is linear—the clip becomes more opaque at a constant rate.

4 In the **Properties** pane, the current properties for the selected keyframe are displayed. In the **Parameters** section, click **More** to see additional parameters.

The **Interpolation** is currently set to **Linear**.

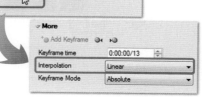

> **💡 Interpolation**
>
> This is a mathematical calculation used to determine the rate of change (the shape of the line) between two keyframes.

Any new keyframe that you add takes its properties from the previous keyframe. (If you select the first keyframe, you will see that its properties are the same.)

5   Click the second keyframe to reselect it and then, in the **Properties** pane, in the **Parameters** section, change the **Interpolation** to **Hold**.

6   On the timeline, in the Opacity envelope strip, click to add a new keyframe. Drag it down to reduce the opacity.

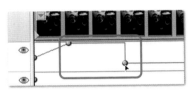

Notice that the blue line between the second and third keyframe is a different shape. This shows a **Hold** interpolation—the opacity remains constant and then changes suddenly. Each interpolation is represented graphically on the envelope strip.

7   Add a fourth keyframe to the envelope strip. This will also have the **Hold** interpolation applied.

8   Preview your clip in the **Video Preview** pane to see the effect.

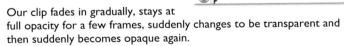

Our clip fades in gradually, stays at full opacity for a few frames, suddenly changes to be transparent and then suddenly becomes opaque again.

What if we want the clip to fade in gradually again rather than the sudden jump? To do this, we need to change the interpolation of the keyframe **before** the change in opacity.

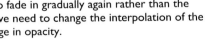

9   Click the third keyframe to select it.

10 In the **Properties** pane, change the **Interpolation** to **Cubic Smooth**.

On the timeline, notice that the
line has changed shape to
represent the new rate of change
in opacity.

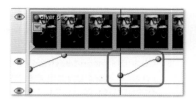

11 Preview your clip in the **Video
Preview** pane to see the effects.

Now that you know how to change opacity using keyframes, let's look at
how to modify an existing preset envelope. This can be a useful technique
as a lot of the hard work of setting up the keyframes is already done for
you!

In this example, we'll create a ghostly effect by modifying the Flicker preset
opacity envelope.

To modify a preset envelope

1 Start a new project and set up the timeline so that it has a
'background' track and an 'overlay'
track as before. Add your
background and overlay clips to the
respective tracks.

2 On the timeline, on your 'overlay'
clip, click the ▼ **Attributes**
button and click **Opacity** in the
drop-down list.

3 On the **Properties** pane, in the **Opacity envelope** section, click
📟Gallery... **Gallery**.

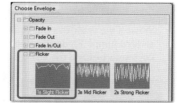

• In the **Choose Envelope** dialog,
click ⊞ to expand the **Flicker**
folder and click to select the **1s
Slight Flicker** thumbnail and then
click **OK**. The envelope is applied
to your clip.

4 Preview your movie to see the
envelope in action. (You might need to press ◄ to 'rewind' the
movie first.)

The preset envelope causes the image to flicker at the beginning of the
clip and then it stays at the same opacity for the remainder of the clip.

5 On the timeline, the keyframes appear as a small cluster. Use the ⊕ **Zoom In** button to zoom in so that you can see the individual keyframes.

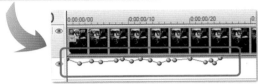

6 Click to select a keyframe and then:

- Drag it towards the top of the strip to increase opacity.

- Drag it towards the bottom of the envelope strip to decrease opacity (increase transparency).

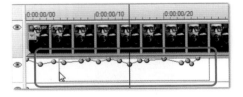

- Drag it to the left or right to change the time and frame at which the opacity is changed.

- Double-click the keyframe to reset the opacity to 100%.

7 Undo any changes by clicking 🔄▾ **Undo** on the Standard toolbar.

8 Click and drag on the envelope strip to select all of the keyframes.

9 Click **Edit > Copy**.

10 Drag on the timeline ruler to set your time indicator to approximately 2 seconds.

11 Click **Edit > Paste**.

12 Preview your clip in the **Video Preview** pane.

Notice that the clip now flickers twice. You can quickly reproduce a complicated effect anywhere on the timeline using this method of copy and paste.

13 To complete the ghostly feel, select the clip and in the **Properties** pane, on the **Properties** tab, change the **Opacity** to 60%.

This step sets the overall opacity—it doesn't change the keyframe settings on the envelope.

> The opacity envelope can be used to adjust any type of clip, including graphic overlays, watermarks and text. For more information about overlays, see the "Overlays" tutorial.
>
> The techniques used to change the keyframes on the opacity envelope also apply to the volume and pan audio envelopes—see the "Audio Techniques" tutorial.
>
> For more information about envelopes in general, see online Help.

What next?

Now that you know the various ways that opacity can be adjusted, it's time to apply these techniques to your projects. A ghost-like special effect is just one of the things you can achieve by using multiple tracks and various opacity settings.

Music and sports videos also work well with this technique, especially when used on a few clips or scenes within the movie. You can use the opacity envelope to animate text and titles, which can bring them to life.

If you're still stuck, there are also plenty of videos on the Internet for you to watch for inspiration. As with any special effects, they often work best when used sparingly.

Have fun!

Masks

Masking is a technique that allows you to hide one part of your video while revealing another. Masks enable you to create special effects or to change the shape of the movie border.

In this tutorial, you'll learn how to:

- Add a simple mask to a track.
- Create a mask from a QuickShape.
- Use video groups to mask one clip and reveal another.

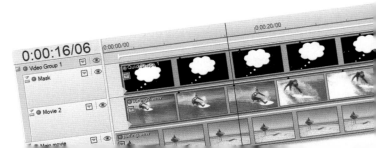

Masks

Masks are used to hide part of a movie or image clip, revealing an alternative clip or background. You can achieve many different effects using masks, for example, you can:

- 'Cut out' a video clip to give it an irregular shaped border.

- Hide part of a clip to make room for text and credits.

- Create special effects, split screen effects or a Picture in Picture by hiding part of a clip and revealing the clip on the track below.

Basic masks

The simplest masks are made up of a white area and a transparent area. When the track is set to a 'mask' blend mode, the white section reveals the clip on the tracks beneath the mask and everything else is hidden. Let's try this now.

To add a mask to a clip

1   Open a new project and add your media to the **Media** pane.

2   Click the 'Video Track 1' header. In the **Properties** pane, in the **Video Track** text box on the **Properties** tab, rename the track to 'Movie'.

3   Click **Insert > Video Track** and in the **Properties** pane, rename this track 'Mask'.

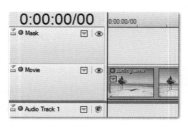

4   Drag your video clip onto the 'Movie' track and crop if necessary.

We've selected a clip where the subject is standing to the left of the picture. This is because we're going to hide the right half of the screen to leave room for our credits.

5   In the **Media** pane, click the **Library** tab to display it. Click ⊞ to expand the **Samples** folder and then click to expand the **Tutorials Workspace** folder. Finally, expand the **Masks** folder and drag the **LeftHalf.png** thumbnail onto the 'Mask' track.

6 Hover the pointer over the right edge of the mask image clip and use the ⇥ **Trim** cursor to extend it to the length of your video clip.

7 With the clip still selected, click ☐Fit **Fit** and choose **Stretch** from the drop-down menu. The white rectangle is stretched to cover half of the preview pane.

8 Click on the header of the 'Mask' track to select it. Then, in the **Properties** pane, in the **Video** section, change the **Blend Mode** to **Mask**.

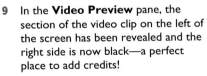

9 In the **Video Preview** pane, the section of the video clip on the left of the screen has been revealed and the right side is now black—a perfect place to add credits!

We assume that you know the basics of adding text to the timeline, so the next steps are really a brief overview. For more information about text formatting, see online Help.

To add credits and adjust the mask start time

1 Insert a new video track above the 'Mask' track and rename it 'Credits'. Then, click to select the 'Credits' track and on the timeline, drag the time indicator to the start time for the credits text clip.

💡 You can nudge your time indicator into exact position on the timeline by using the arrow keys on your keyboard.

2 Click  and type your credit text. Position the text object to the right of the **Video Preview** pane, in line with the black rectangle. We used the **Properties** pane to format our credits and set text **Scrolling** to **Up**.

3 Hover the mouse pointer over the right edge of the text clip and use the ⊏⊡⊐ **Trim** cursor to extend the clip to the end of the movie.

Now, all that's left to do is to change the point where the mask comes into effect.

4 Hover the mouse pointer over the left edge of the mask image clip and use the ⊏⊡⊐ **Trim** cursor to drag the clip to the new start position, just before the start of the credit text.

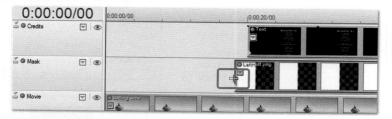

5 Finally, preview the effect in the **Video Preview** pane. (You might need to press ⏮ to 'rewind' the movie first.)

Notice that the movie plays at full size and then the mask appears, followed by your scrolling credit text.

This is because the mask track only alters the underlying track when it contains a clip. Where the track is empty, the underlying tracks will not be affected.

Advanced masking

So far, we have added a mask to tracks that are all on the same level on the timeline. This means that any clip that is on a track below the mask track will be affected. So, how do we create the effect where one clip plays alongside the other? If we just add another track beneath the mask track, both tracks will be affected by the mask. The answer is to use **video groups**. Let's try this now.

To use a mask to display two movie or image clips you need a video group and a minimum of three video tracks: two for movie or image clips, one for the mask.

To set up a video group for a mask

1   Open a new project and add your media to the **Media** pane.

2   Click the 'Video Track 1' header. In the **Properties** pane, in the **Video Track** text box on the **Properties** tab, rename the track 'Main movie'.

3   Click **Insert > Video Track** to insert two additional tracks and rename these 'Movie 2' and 'Mask'.

4   Click **Insert > Video Group**. In the **Properties** pane, in the **Video Track** text box on the **Properties** tab, rename the group 'Mask group'.

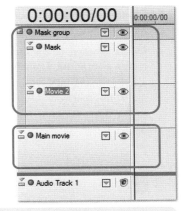

5   Click the 'Mask' track header to select it and then, click **Arrange > Move Into Group**. Repeat for the 'Movie 2' track.

Your timeline should look like the one illustrated.

Key points:

*   The 'Mask' track is above the 'Movie 2' track and both are inside the group.

*   The 'Main movie' track is not in the group.

If necessary, rearrange the track order using the **Arrange** menu.

Shortcut keys are displayed in the menu next to the command or on the tooltip on the button. For example, **Ctrl+Up** moves the selected track up the track order.

To use a mask within a video group

1 Drag your video (or image) clip onto the 'Main movie' track and crop as necessary.

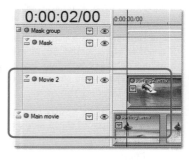

2 Drag your second video clip onto the 'Movie 2' track, so that it starts 2 seconds after the main clip.

3 Add a crop and transform as necessary to roughly position your clip in the upper right corner.

4 Click to select the 'Mask' track and position the time indicator at 2 seconds—in line with the start time of the 'Movie 2' clip.

5 Click **Insert > CG clip > QuickShape.**

6 In the **Properties** pane, on the **Properties** tab, use the drop-down menu to change the **QuickShape type** to **Thought Bubble**.

7 On the timeline, on the QuickShape 1 clip, click the ⬇ **Attributes** button and choose **Transform** from the drop-down menu.

Position the QuickShape in the **Video Preview** pane so that it sits on top of the 'Movie 2' clip.

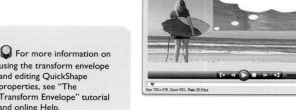

💡 For more information on using the transform envelope and editing QuickShape properties, see "The Transform Envelope" tutorial and online Help.

8 On the timeline, drag the right edge of the QuickShape clip so that it matches the length of your 'Movie 2' clip.

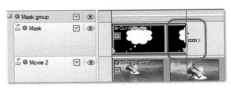

9 Click the 'Mask' track header to select the track, then, in the **Properties** pane, in the **Video** section, change the **Blend Mode** to **Mask**.

10 Preview your movie in the **Video Preview** pane to see the effect. (You might need to press [image] to 'rewind' the movie first.)

The 'Movie 2' clip is now cut out into the shape of a thought bubble. This effect works with any QuickShape as long as it is coloured white.

Other mask examples

You can create masks from a variety of different images, and even from video clips. They work best with clips that have solid white areas and transparent sections. However, you can also create interesting effects by using coloured masks, text or even photos! Because the mask blend mode is set on the track, it means that the clip used as the mask can have keyframe animations, effects and transitions.

The following examples should give you some ideas. The techniques used are the same—they all have a track set to mask blend mode and use a video group to contain the mask—but the result is very different.

Example 1 - Title mask

We added visual interest to our diving movie opening title sequence by using the title text itself as a mask.

To create the title sequence, on the timeline we added a 'Title animation' video group containing three video tracks—the title 'mask' track, an overlay, and a background track.

We then added a text clip to the uppermost track. The text was formatted with a large, bold font and resized to fill the **Video Preview** pane. We also applied a 'Left' scrolling animation. Finally, in the **Properties** pane, we set the blend mode on the track to '**Mask**'.

The main video clip was set to start after the title sequence had finished. The blank area on the 'Main movie' video track created an effective, black background for the title.

As you can see from the timeline screenshot above, the movie begins with the title sequence before the movie fades in.

Example 2 - Custom image masks

This example illustrates some of the different effects that you can achieve using a custom mask. We used three similar PNG images—all with transparent areas. In each case, the main movie shows through the transparent area.

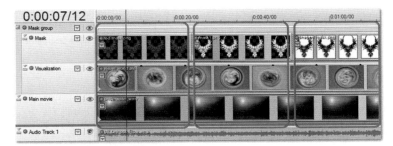

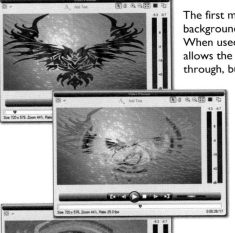

The first mask has a transparent background with a red line art image. When used as a mask, the red image allows the underlying clip to show through, but tints it red.

The second mask is more conventional. It has a transparent background with a white line art image. The underlying clip is untinted.

The third mask is an inverse of the second—the image background is white and the line art image is transparent.

> In the **Media** pane on the **Library** tab, the **Tutorials Workspace** folder contains two shaped masks for you to experiment with. These were created in our image editing software, Serif PhotoPlus. If you want to create your own masks, make sure that you export the image files as 24 or 32 bit PNGs to preserve any transparent areas.

Knowing how to use masks is a useful skill. Ever wondered how the same actor plays both twins simultaneously in a movie? Most likely, the effect was created using two cleverly filmed video clips and a mask.

For more ideas, take a look at the other tutorials in this section; in particular the "Split Screen" and "Picture in Picture" tutorials as both of these effects can be achieved or enhanced by using a mask track. You could also experiment with the transform envelope and animate your mask to achieve some amazing effects.

> Why not combine the masking technique with clip extending to add interest to your credits? See the "Extending Clips" tutorial for more information.

The Split Screen

As its name suggests, the split screen is a technique in which two or more movie or image clips are displayed simultaneously on different parts of the screen.

This effect is popular in many TV shows and sports channels and can be used as a way of adding drama or to display action simultaneously. For example, you could show both sides of a telephone call; show the action from the sports race leaders; or use it as a way of leading into another related video clip.

In this tutorial, you'll learn how to create a split screen effect using preset transforms.

The Split Screen

The next few steps will introduce you to the split screen by applying a transform to a single keyframe at a track level. However, the same techniques can also be applied to clips, and over multiple keyframes to achieve some spectacular effects.

To create a 4-way split screen effect

1   Add your media to the media pane (ideally, you will need four clips to complete the effect) and switch to Timeline mode if necessary.

2   Click **Insert > Video track** and insert three more tracks so that you have four in total.

    Resize the timeline by dragging the top edge so that you can see all of the tracks at the same time.

3   Drag a clip to each of the video tracks.

    Don't worry that you can't see all of your clips in the **Video Preview** pane, we'll come to that in a minute.

    Each clip needs to be changed in size and position.

    We could do this manually using the **transform envelope** on each clip—sometimes this can create a great custom effect. However, let's make MoviePlus do the hard work for us and use one of the preset transforms.

4   On Video Track 4, click the
    🔽 **Attributes** button and click Transform in the drop-down list.

> 💡 Shortcut keys are available for many of the common tasks. For example, the **F9** key adds a new video track. The shortcut key is either displayed in the menu next to the command or on the tooltip on the button.

5 In the **Properties** pane, in the **Transform envelope** section, click .

6 In the **Choose Envelope** dialog, click to expand the **Split Screen** folder, then click to expand the **Quad** folder and choose **Quad Top-Left**. Click **OK**.

7 Follow steps 4 - 6 to apply different 'Quad' transforms—**Quad Top-Right, Quad Bottom-Right** and **Quad Bottom-Left**—to each video track.

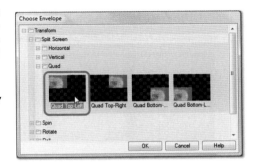

8 Preview your movie from the start. You should see all of your clips playing simultaneously.

For more information about using the transform and more ideas for using multiple clips simultaneously, see the "Transform Envelope" and "Picture in Picture" tutorials. To create other split screen effects, see the "Masks" tutorial.

Finishing touches

To complete the effect, there are a few more things you could do, for example:

- Add background music or mute all other audio apart from one track.
- Apply a crop to each movie or image clip using ▭Ft to refine the look and remove any black borders. (Or even modify each clip's transform envelope to add black borders!)

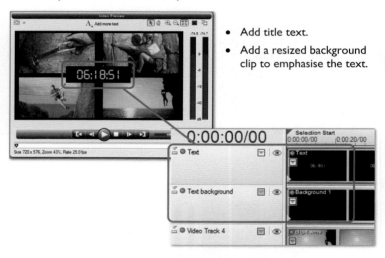

- Add title text.
- Add a resized background clip to emphasise the text.

Picture in Picture

The Picture in Picture (PiP) technique can be used to add fun effects to your movies or slideshows. For example, PiP can be used to display different camera angles simultaneously or show closeups of the star sportsman as well as the entire game. PiP has its uses for tutorial style videos too!

In this tutorial, you'll learn how to:

- Create a simple PiP effect using only two video tracks.
- Create a custom shaped PiP effect using a mask.

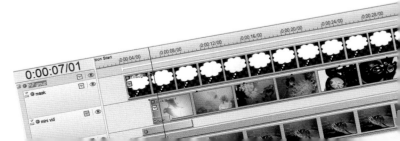

Picture in Picture (PiP)

The Picture in Picture effect looks really impressive and can create an element of fun. Although it can take on many forms, the techniques used to create the PiP in MoviePlus are very similar.

The first part of this tutorial will show you how to do this using only two video tracks and a transform; the second part will create a shaped PiP video clip. This is a little more involved, but looks great. Follow the steps in the tutorial and you will soon be a master of Picture in Picture.

To create a simple PiP effect

1   Open a new project, switch to Timeline mode, and then add your media to the **Media** pane. At the very least, you will need two image or video clips. (The tutorial will refer to video clips from now on but you may use either.)

2   Drag your background (main) video clip to Video Track 1.

3   Click the track header and then, in the **Properties** pane, on the **Properties** tab, rename the track 'Background'.

4   Click ⬚ Fit⌄ and choose **Custom** from the drop-down menu. Crop your image to fit the **Video Preview** pane.

5   Click the 'Background' track header and then click **Insert > Video Track**. In the **Properties** pane, on the **Properties** tab, rename this new track to 'PiP track'. Check that this track is **above** the 'Background' track. If not, use the **Arrange** menu to reorder the tracks.

6 Click the Audio Track 1 header and then click **Insert > Audio Track**.
A new audio track is inserted above Audio Track 1.

7 Click and drag on the timeline ruler to set the time indicator to 5
seconds. (You can nudge it into exact position by using the arrow
keys.) This leaves time before the PiP effect to add a transition, or
allows you to add title text to the movie.

8 Drag your PiP video clip
from the **Media** pane to
the 'PiP' track. As the clip
gets close to the time
indicator, it 'snaps' into
position.

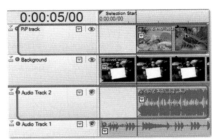

Notice that the PiP audio
has been placed on Audio
Track 2.

If you preview your movie in the
Video Preview pane, you will see
that the second video clip starts 5
seconds into your movie, but it
obscures the background video clip.

Let's change the size of the second clip
to create the PiP effect.

The size of the clip is changed using the **transform envelope**.
However, as we want all clips on the 'PiP track' to be the same size
and in the same place, it is best to apply the transform to the track
header.

9 On the PiP track header,
click the ▼ **Attributes**
button. The button has
changed to ▼ to show
that a new transform
envelope is open. If you
can't see the envelope
strip, use the scroll bars or
resize your timeline.

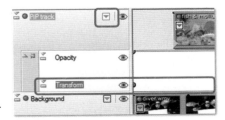

10 In the **Video Preview** pane, resize and reposition the clip to the desired location. To change the aspect ratio, press the **Shift** key when resizing the bounding box.

11 Preview your movie to see the effect. (You might need to press [image] to 'rewind' the movie first.)

> For a simple PiP effect, you can use the preset transforms.
>
> With the transform envelope selected, in the **Properties** pane, click [Gallery] and replace your transform with one of the **Quad** presets.

PiP audio

If you have used two video clips, you may notice that the audio plays for both clips at the same time. There are several ways that you can approach this:

- Mute only the unwanted audio track.

  - or -

- Apply a volume envelope to the audio clips (or tracks) so that you can 'blend' the clips together.

  - or -

- Mute the original audio track(s) and insert a new audio track for background music or narration.

It is also possible that the audio can end up on the same track. In this case:

- Insert a new audio track (if necessary), drag one of the audio clips to the new track and then mute the unwanted audio track.

(See the "Audio Techniques" tutorial for more information about managing audio clips.)

To add title text

1   On the timeline ruler, drag the time indicator to the start of the movie (0:00:00/00).

2   Click to select the 'PiP' track and then click `A Insert Text Clip`.

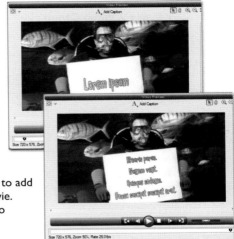

A text clip is inserted at the beginning of the movie and is already positioned for the PiP effect.

3   Use the **Properties** pane to format the text.

4   Drag the time indicator to the end of the 'PiP' video clip and click `A Insert Text Clip` to add text to the end of your movie. Use the **Properties** pane to format the text as before.

5   Preview your movie from the start to see your changes.

> 💡 For that extra special touch, don't forget to use transitions and animations on some of your clips. However, remember the golden rule: transitions and animations can look great, but don't overuse them!

We can refine the look of the PiP effect by adding a mask. A mask enables us to completely change the shape of the small video, without affecting any other properties. The steps are summarized below.

> ℹ For step-by-step instructions on setting up groups and mask tracks, see the "Masks" tutorial.

To create a custom shaped PiP

1 Select the 'PiP' track and click **Insert > Video** track.

2 In the **Properties** pane, rename the new track 'Mask'.

3 Click **Insert > Video Group**.

4 Click the track header to select the 'Mask' track and click **Arrange > Move into Group** (or you could use the shortcut keys **Ctrl+Right**).

5 Select the 'PiP' track and click **Arrange > Move into Group**.

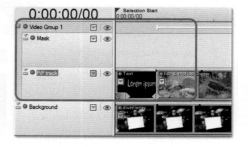

The 'PiP' track should be below the 'Mask' track. If not, use the **Arrange** menu to rearrange it (or use **Ctrl+Up** or **Down**).

The 'Background' track **must** remain outside the group.

6 Select the 'Mask' track and on the timeline ruler, drag to position the time indicator at 0:00:00/00.

7 Click **Insert > QuickShape** and use the **Trim** cursor to extend the QuickShape clip to the length of your movie.

> 🔍 **Learn shortcuts!**
>
> Shortcut keys are available for many of the common tasks. For example, the **F9** key adds a new video track, **F11** adds a video group. The shortcut key is either displayed in the menu next to the command or on the tooltip on the button.

8 On the QuickShape clip, click the 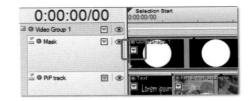 **Attributes** button and click **Transform** in the drop-down list.

9 Resize the QuickShape in the **Video Preview** pane and position it so that it covers the PiP clip.

10 Click to select the 'Mask' track header and in the **Properties** pane, on the **Properties** tab, set the **Blend mode** to **Mask**.

11 Finally, preview the finished PiP effect in the **Video Preview** pane. (You might need to press ▐◀ to 'rewind' the movie first.)

Using these techniques, you can create some really impressive Picture in Picture effects. This effect can also be used at any point in a movie—just move the clips to a different point on the timeline.

Above all, have fun experimenting!

Audio Techniques

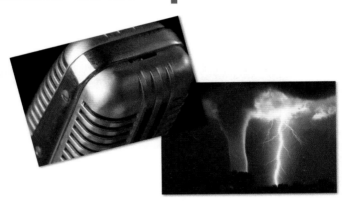

To make a movie interesting, you're going to need some sort of sound. This tutorial looks at how you can use multiple audio tracks to add special effects, narration and background sound.

In this tutorial, you'll learn how to:

- Combine multiple audio tracks.
- Enhance your audio by applying sound effects.
- Work with audio envelopes.

Audio Techniques

Great movies all have one thing in common, a great soundtrack. Sound adds impact to a movie, even if you don't realise it at the time. A good background track, perhaps combined with narration, can also add interest to slideshows and helps to keep your audience's attention.

Our tutorial example uses a static image clip that is 2.5 minutes long. We modified a 'flicker' opacity envelope to produce an effect like lightning. The 'flicker' keyframes begin at 32 seconds and are reproduced at various points within the clip. To see how this is done, see the "Fading In and Out" tutorial.

We'll create our audio from scratch using various audio clips. This will introduce you to the various audio techniques and effects that you can apply to your future projects.

Before we add any audio to the timeline, we'll give you a quick introduction to **markers**. These provide a visual reference to key points on the timeline, and can be used as a visual guide to help line up clips or keyframes. Markers are particularly useful when working with multiple tracks. In our example, we've used a marker to indicate the 'lightning flicker' (opacity envelope keyframes) so that we can line up our audio clips.

To insert timeline markers

1   On the timeline, drag the time indicator to position it at 32 seconds (in our case, the first cluster of 'lightning' flicker opacity keyframes on the clip).

2   On the context toolbar, click ▷ Marker and choose **Insert Marker** from the drop-down list.

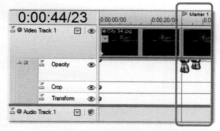

A green marker displays on the timeline.

Although you can layer multiple audio clips on one audio track, it's easier to see what's going on when overlapping clips have their own track. (It also allows you to apply different effects to each clip.) Adding multiple audio tracks is virtually the same as adding extra video tracks, so these steps should feel really familiar.

Markers are visible even when tracks are minimized. This allows you to line up clips or keyframes on multiple tracks.

To create multiple audio tracks and add clips

1 Click **Insert > Audio** track (or press the **F10** key).

A new audio track is inserted above Audio Track 1.

Repeat step 1 to add another audio track, so that you have three audio tracks in total.

Now, let's add some audio clips!

2 In the **Media** pane, click the **Library** tab to display it. Click ⊞ to expand the **Samples** folder and then click to expand the **Tutorials Workspace** folder. Finally, expand the **Audio** folder.

3 Drag **Rainshower.wma** onto Audio Track 1.

4 In the **Properties** pane, on the **Properties** tab, select the **Enable Clip Extending** check box and select the **Loop** option.

5 On the timeline, hover over the edge of the clip and with the
⁺ₘₘ⟩ **Extend clip** cursor, click and drag the edge of the clip to the right.

We extended our clip so that it plays for the entire length of our video clip.

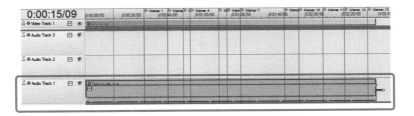

Looping Audio

Although MoviePlus can loop a clip for you, you can sometimes achieve a more natural effect by dragging multiple instances of the clip to the timeline and overlapping them slightly. This can often smooth out small 'gaps' in the audio caused by the MP3 or WMA compression format. (WAV files are 'gapless' files and will loop seamlessly without any modification.)

Don't forget that you can also trim a clip before looping it. See online Help for information about trimming clips.

For more information about extending clips, see the "Extending Clips" tutorial.

6 Preview your movie in the **Video preview** pane.

7 On the timeline, drag the time indicator to 1 second. Use the arrow keys to nudge the time indicator into exact position.

8 Drag the **crowclose.wma** clip from the **Audio** folder onto Audio Track 2. Notice how it snaps to the time indicator when it gets close to it.

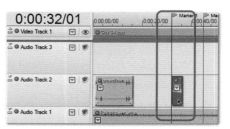

9 Drag the **Thunder.wma** clip from the **Audio** folder onto Audio Track 2 and position it next to your first marker. This also snaps into place.

Repeat the step to add several more thunder sound clips to Audio Track 2.

10 Finally, on the timeline, drag the time indicator to approximately 21 seconds. Drag the **clockstrikesmidnight.wma** clip from the **Library** tab on the **Media** pane onto Audio Track 3.

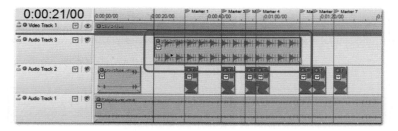

11 Preview your movie in the **Video preview** pane. (You might need to press 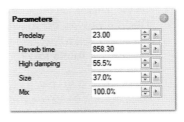 to 'rewind' the movie first.)

You'll notice that because we've used multiple instances of the same audio clip, the audio sounds a little repetitive. What can we do about it? Let's apply some sound effects to add a little 'colour.'

To add effects to an audio clip

1 On the timeline, click to select the first **Thunder.wma** clip on Audio Track 2.

2 In the **Properties** pane, on the **Effects** tab, click **Add Effect...**

3 In the **Choose Effect** dialog, click **Reverb** and click **OK**.

4 On the timeline, set the time indicator to a few seconds before the start of the clip. Preview the effect in the **Video Preview** pane.

5 In the **Properties** pane, on the **Effects** tab, scroll down to the **Parameters** section. Adjust the effects settings and preview the clip to hear the effect.

There are no set values for the different sound effects, it is really a case of trial and error. In general, the higher you set the value, the more obvious the effect.

Parameters		
Predelay	23.00	
Reverb time	858.30	
High damping	55.5%	
Size	37.0%	
Mix	100.0%	

6 To create varied thunder sounds, apply different settings to each of the **Thunder.wma** clips.

You can add several sound effects to a clip at once. Try some of the other sound effects and preview the results. If you add something that you don't like, you can always delete it.

When adding sound effects to your clips, it is often useful to mute the other audio tracks. You can turn mute on and off by clicking 🔘 on the track header.

Next, let's change the sound by changing the duration of an audio clip.

To create an effect by changing the clip duration

1 On the timeline, click to select a **Thunder.wma** clip on Audio track 2.

2 Hover over the right edge of the clip, press the **Ctrl** key on the keyboard, and then drag the edge to the right so that the clip gets longer.

3 Preview the effect in the **Video Preview** pane.

The thunder clip lasts longer and the pitch sounds a lot deeper. If you **Ctrl**-drag the clip to make it shorter, the pitch will get higher. This effect works better for some sounds than it does for others.

Finally, let's change the audio using the volume and pan envelopes. The envelopes can be applied at group, track or clip level. As we have lots of individual clips, we're going to apply the envelopes to the track.

To move audio from left to right using the pan envelope

1 On the timeline, on the Audio Track 2 header, click the 🔽 **Attributes** button and select **Pan** from the drop-down list. The envelope strip opens.

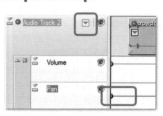

The first keyframe is positioned in the centre of the strip. This shows that the audio is in the centre—it plays at an equal volume through both speakers.

2 Click to select the first keyframe and in the **Properties** pane, change the **Interpolation** to **Hold**.

3 On the timeline, drag the time indicator to the start of the **crowclose.wma** clip. Hover the mouse pointer over the envelope strip, close to the time indicator, until you see the ➕ cursor.

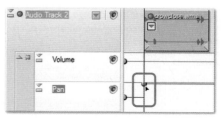

Click to insert a keyframe and drag it to the top of the envelope strip.

4 Drag the time indicator to the start of the first **Thunder.wma** clip. Insert a keyframe and drag it to the bottom of the envelope strip.

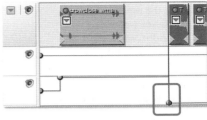

5 Press to 'rewind' the movie and preview the effect in the **Video preview** pane.

You will notice that the crow sounds come from the left speaker and the thunder comes from the right. All of the other sounds are in the centre of the speakers.

Add more keyframes to the pan envelope strip and experiment with the keyframe position. You can also change the **interpolation** type to get the sound to pan gradually from one speaker to the other.

To change the volume on the track

1 **Optional:** On the timeline, on the Audio Track 2 header, click the **Attributes** button and select **Volume** from the drop-down list. The envelope strip opens.

2 Drag the time indicator to the start of the first **Thunder.wma** clip. Insert a keyframe and drag it down slightly.

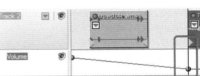

The closer the keyframe is to the bottom of the strip, the quieter the sound of the clip.

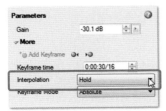

3 With the keyframe still selected (highlighted red), in the **Properties** pane, change the **Interpolation** to **Hold**.

> **Interpolation**
>
> This is a mathematical calculation used to determine the rate of change (the shape of the line) between two keyframes.

4   Drag the time indicator
     to the start of the next
     Thunder.wma clip,
     insert a keyframe and
     drag it towards the top
     of the clip.

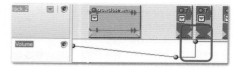

5   Press to 'rewind' the movie and preview the effect in the **Video preview** pane.

As the movie plays, the crows will sound as if they are moving further away as the volume decreases slowly. The first roll of thunder will be quiet and distant sounding. Because we applied **Hold** interpolation to the second keyframe, the volume will suddenly increase, making the second thunder clip loud. This will give the impression that the storm is overhead.

Experiment with the volume envelope—add more keyframes and change the interpolation to create different effects.

As you can see, there is so much you can do with audio, and we have only touched on the basics! The online Help contains information about using **effects groups** to give you even more control over your audio effects.

As with any effect, some things you try will work, other's won't. But you can still have a lot of fun finding out. Good luck!

> You can use the volume envelope to fade (alternate) the audio between tracks. This is done by applying a volume envelope to each track. The keyframes are set at the same time, but at high volume on one envelope, and at low volume on the other.

> The volume and pan envelopes work in the same way as the opacity envelope on a video track—you change the envelope by inserting keyframes on the envelope strip. For a more detailed explanation, see the "Fading In and Out" tutorial.

DVD/VCD Menu Templates

When you've finished editing your movie, open Menu Designer and browse the wide selection of themed DVD/VCD menu templates that are included with MoviePlus. All templates can be customized, so you're sure to find something to suit your needs.

The templates are categorized as follows:

- General
- Animated
- Kids and Baby
- Holiday and Festivities
- Wedding and Romance
- Seasons
- Funky
- Moods
- Sports
- Antique
- Movie Styles
- Home
- Modern
- Celebrations

For details on customizing the templates, see the **How To** pane or online Help.

General

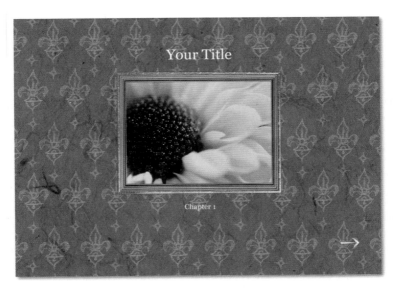

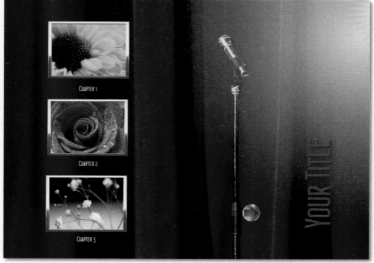

Animated

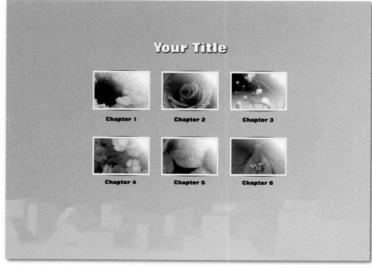

Kids and Baby

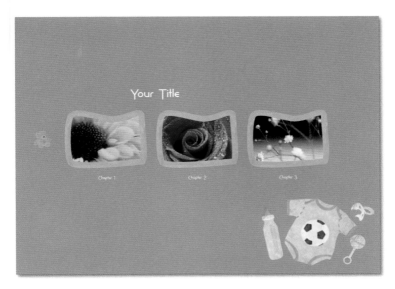

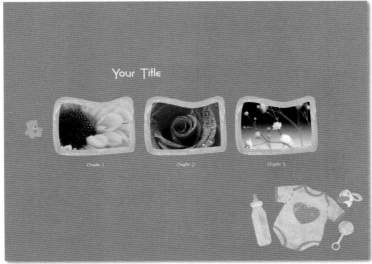

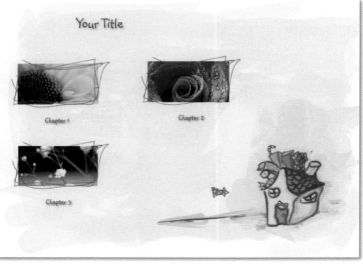

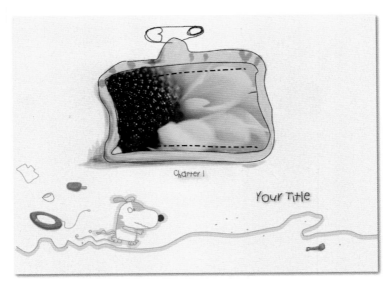

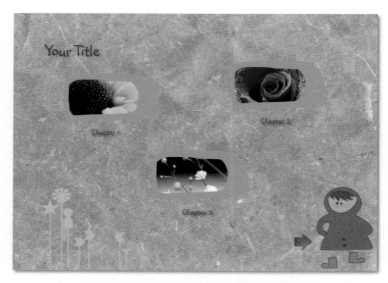

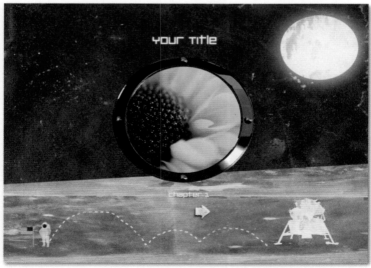

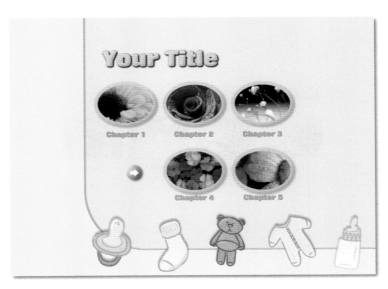

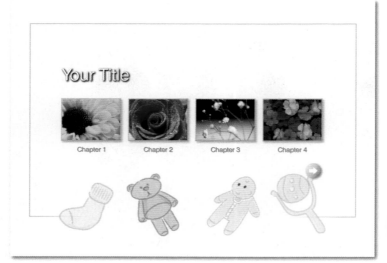

Holiday and Festivities

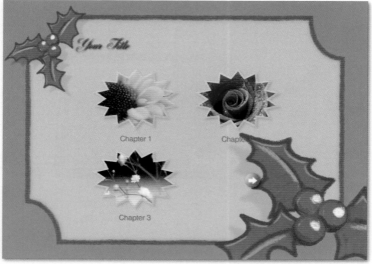

Wedding and Romance

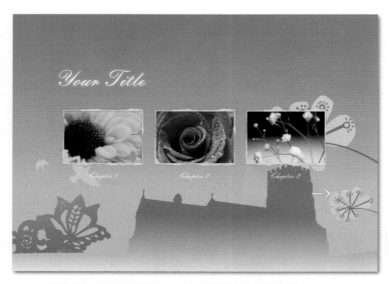

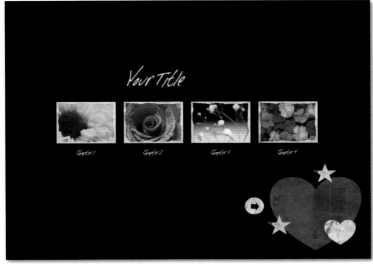

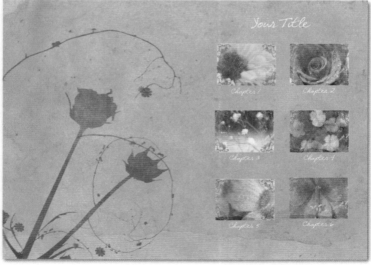

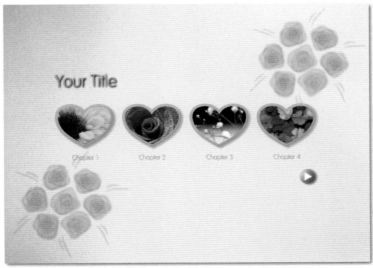

Seasons

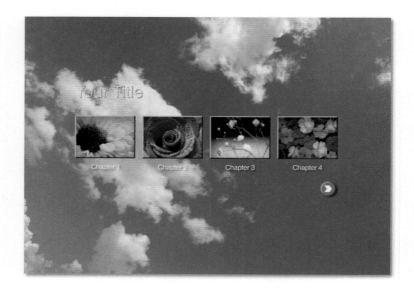

Funky

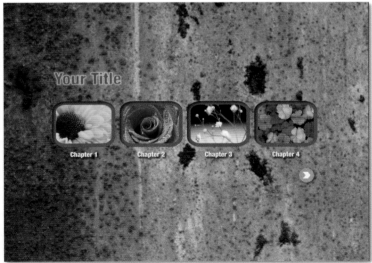

Your Title

Chapter 1   Chapter 2   Chapter 3   Chapter 4

Moods

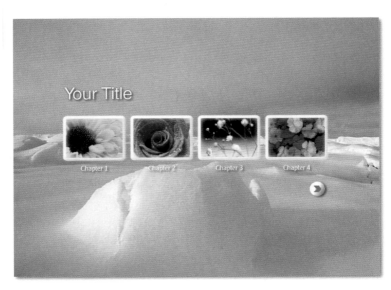

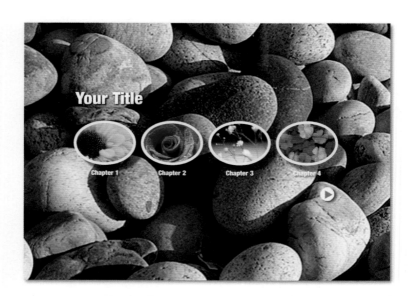

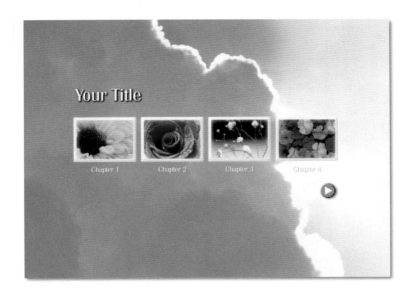

Sports

Antique

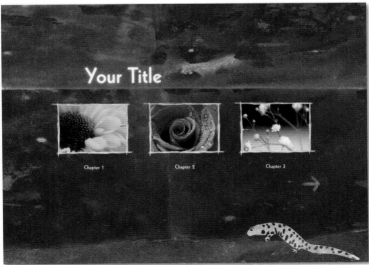

Movie Styles

Home

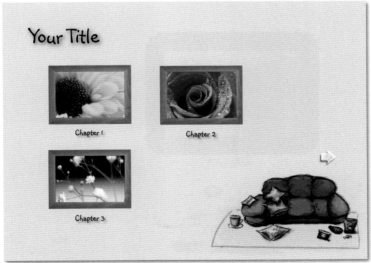

Modern

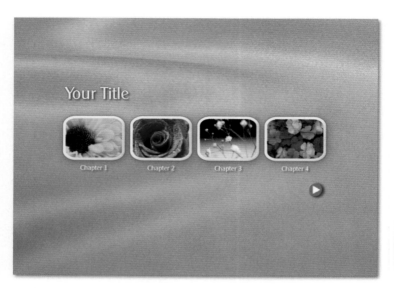

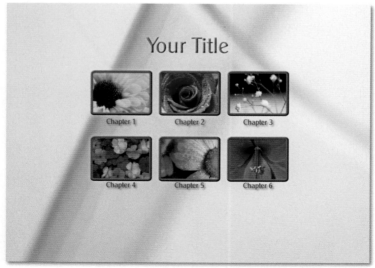

Celebrations

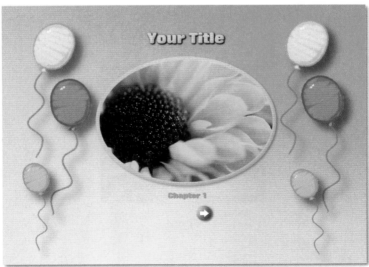

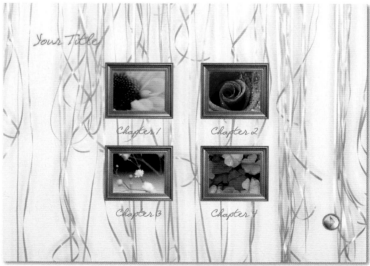

Glossary

audio track

In MoviePlus, a track on the timeline containing an audio clip.

Also used to refer to the area of a videotape that is used for recording the audio information accompanying a video clip.

blue screening

See *chroma key*.

capture card/capture device

Internal or external device that connects analogue media devices (such as a VCR or analogue video camcorder) to a computer, and converts the input from the device into digital format.

Internal devices (capture cards) fit into a PCI slot on your computer's motherboard, external devices generally attach via USB port.

capturing

The process of converting video footage and associated audio from an analogue source (such as a VHS tape) to digital format. See also *capture card*.

chapter point

A type of marker used to define the beginning of the various chapters in your movie.

chroma key

A method of removing a colour (or colour range) from one video clip or image to reveal another clip or image behind it. The 'removed' colour becomes transparent. Also known as *blue screening*.

codec

Software that compresses and decompresses audio and video data streams.

downloading

In MoviePlus, the process of importing video footage directly from a digital source (such as a camcorder with a DVD drive, hard drive, memory card, or non-removable flash memory) onto a computer.

effect

Used to add visual interest to your movie, or to correct or enhance the original image. MoviePlus effect presets include Greyscale, Colourize, Brightness/Contrast, Gaussian Blur, etc.

envelope

(Timeline mode only)

A method of applying change to a video or audio clip over time. MoviePlus provides various envelopes that work in similar ways to control properties such as opacity, volume, crop, and so on.

exporting

The process of converting a movie to a file format that others can view.

fade

Refers to changes in the volume of an audio clip. (See also *gain*.)

FireWire

An external transmission path that supports very fast data transfer rates. Particularly suitable for connecting digital video devices to the computer. (Also referred to as IEEE 1394.)

gain

Refers to the overall volume of an audio clip. (See also *fade*.)

IEEE 1394

See *FireWire*.

Ken Burns effect

Named after the documentary filmmaker Ken Burns, this technique uses *pan and zoom* effects to give the impression of movement to still images. The stills are often embedded in video clips with *fade transitions* between them.

keyframe

(Timeline mode only)

In MoviePlus, keyframes are used to record changes to a video/audio clip over time. Each keyframe marks the start of a particular change, such as the application of an *effect* or *envelope*.

mask

(Timeline mode only)

Masks are generally used to 'cut out' a shaped portion from a video clip, effectively removing a background to give focus to a foreground element.

pan and zoom

A technique that involves panning across a scene and zooming into a subject of interest to add dynamic impact. See also *Ken Burns effect*.

rippling

Rippling helps to keep the position of video and audio clips constant in relation to one another, saving you the effort of manoeuvring multiple clips each time you make a minor edit. To enable rippling in MoviePlus, use the **Rippling** button on the Context toolbar. (For details, see online Help.)

scrub

To move back and forth through your movie using the preview slider or time indicator.

storyboard

(Storyboard mode only)

Traditionally, a visual script of the scenes and scene changes in a series of video shots. In MoviePlus, you'll use the storyboard in a similar way, adding video and audio clips, *transitions*, *effects*, and so on, to gradually build up the scenes of your movie. (Advanced users may prefer to use the *timeline*.)

timeline

(Timeline mode only)

The timeline represents the flow of a movie from start to finish. It consists of stacked layers of video, audio, images, titles and credits clips, and so on.

transition

A gradual way of switching from one scene to another. A transition can appear at the start (In transition) or end (Out transition) of a scene.

trimming

A technique that refers to adjusting the in and/or out points of a video or audio clip.

USB

Short for Universal Serial Bus. A way to connect a computer to devices such as digital cameras, keyboards, printers, external video *capture devices*, etc. Connection occurs via a USB port on the computer, either directly to the device, or through a USB cable.

video track

In MoviePlus, a track on the timeline containing video clips, still images, text clips, etc.

Also used to refer to the area of the videotape used for recording the video information.